Speaking, Listening and Drama

Andy Kempe and Jan Holroyd

David Fulton Publishers

Related Titles

Beginning Drama 11–14 (second edition), Jonothan Neelands
ISBN: 1–84312–086–0
Starting Drama Teaching, Mike Fleming
ISBN: 1–85346–788–X

David Fulton Publishers Ltd
The Chiswick Centre, 414 Chiswick High Road, London W4 5TF

www.fultonpublishers.co.uk

First published in Great Britain in 2004 by David Fulton Publishers

10 9 8 7 6 5 4 3 2 1

Note: The right of the authors to be identified as the authors of this work has been asserted by them in accordance with the Copyright, Designs and Patents Act 1988.

David Fulton Publishers is a division of Granada Learning Limited, part of the Granada plc.

Copyright © Andy Kempe and Jan Holroyd 2004

British Library Cataloguing in Publication Data
A catalogue record for this book is available from the British Library.

ISBN 1 84312 041 0

Typeset by RefineCatch Limited, Bungay, Suffolk
Printed and bound in Great Britain by The Thanet Press, Margate

Contents

Acknowledgements

THE AUTHORS WOULD like to express their gratitude to the following people who have contributed to this book: Alan Murray, Alice Evans, Alison Green, Eve Bearne, Dr Helen Nicholson, Marigold Ashwell, Ron Carter, Samm Line, June Hurst, past and present students on the PGCE Secondary Drama course at the University of Reading, English and drama teachers involved in the University of Reading Schools Partnership and pupils at John Rankin Junior, Park House and Denefield Schools in West Berkshire.

Language and learning

Introduction

WHAT VOICE DO you hear in your head as you read this? Is it your own, or are you ascribing a voice to us, the writers? Perhaps you are reading in a different way altogether, skimming for general sense or scanning for particular words. We are absent from your experience. We have little control over how you read this text. One of us is male, the other female. We both have regional accents, one from Lancashire, one from London. We both come from working/lower middle class backgrounds and were state educated. Does knowing this alter the way you are reading? Does it change the sense of it? What is certain is that if we were telling you all this face to face it would.

Speaking and listening involves presence. It involves performing and interpreting performance. If we were talking to you 'live' then we could help you to scan our text by emphasising key words and, by varying the pace of our delivery, affect the way you skim over some points while dwelling on others. But it wouldn't just be one-way traffic. While presenting our ideas we would doubtless be scanning your face and posture for signs that we were being heard and understood. We would adapt our performance accordingly. Well, at least, as students and teachers of language, we would hope that we'd be able to do this! What we do know is that neither our performance nor the way it might be interpreted will be free from value judgements and prejudice. In a live oral interaction, it is not just what we say that carries weight, but how we say it and what we are doing while we are saying it. The way we speak gives us social capital. But let's be clear, as with economic capital, exchange rates can fluctuate. Speech that may be highly valued in one context can be an encumbrance in another time and place. In the same way that the way we dress, move and position ourselves in space says a lot about us, so the act of speaking reveals something of our identity, regionality, class, background and temporal existence. To criticise the way someone speaks is to criticise them.

This book aims to help English and drama teachers to work towards ensuring that children are taught to speak and listen effectively: that is, to be able to say what they want in ways that will have the result they want, and to derive benefit from what they are listening to. Such a project involves challenging the very possibility of assessing pupils' performance without attending to both the visual and aural signifiers that accompany live oral communication and the value systems that affect how what is said is received and interpreted. Inevitably, the notion of standard English will need to be discussed. One argument that will be considered is that the use of standard English in its spoken form can negate prejudice attached to class, race, regionality and gender. Another argument is that standard English endows all children with an equal amount of social capital (how they choose to use it of course being up to them). Conversely, 'standard English' may be regarded as a manifestation of a dominant social model that legitimises some types of speech and devalues others. Consideration must therefore be given to what constitutes standard spoken English, what values are attached to the term and how an understanding of these issues may enhance the development of children's ability to use language effectively.

The rise and realities of oracy in the classroom

Most children first encounter language in its spoken form. This is true even for children who are hearing-impaired, who experience the visual if not all of the aural elements of live oral communication. The task of the teacher is to build on this experience of talk as a means of discovering, exploring and developing the child's perception of the world and ablility, subsequently, to communicate this through their own use of spoken and written language. In the 1960s, as liberal humanist ideals began to dominate the educational landscape, the ability to articulate thought and feeling, or lack of it, was been seen as having personal, social and economic consequences. The Newsom Report of 1963 emotively identified a gulf between those who had, and the many who had not, sufficient command of words to be able to listen and discuss rationally; to express ideas and feelings clearly; and even to have ideas at all. The report admitted to simply not knowing how many people were frustrated by an inability to express themselves adequately or develop intellectually because they lacked the words with which to think and reason. Such a matter was, at the time, seen as being of equal importance to economic life and personal living given that failures in industrial relations, as well as marriages, resulted from failures in communications (DES 1963).

This line of thought led to a study being commissioned to investigate the extent to which schools were equipping young people for life outside the classroom. Entitled *A Language for Life* (the Bullock Report), it concluded that oral language was vitally important to the teaching of English on the grounds that:

> As a consumer, a worker, a voter, a member of his community, each person has pressing reasons for being able to evaluate the words of others. He has equally pressing reasons for making his own voice heard. Too many people lack the ability to do either with confidence. Too many are unable to speak articulately in any context which might test their security. The result can be acquiescence, apathy or a dependence upon entrenched and unexamined prejudices.

> (DES 1975: 140)

However, while the Bullock Report made clear recommendations about what should be done to improve the teaching of spoken language skills, a study four years later (HMI 1979) reported that English teachers were still reluctant to use oral work as a method of learning. Used to written exercises, dictation and reading by rote, they were suspicious of speaking and listening work, which could seem ephemeral in nature and outcome. And although Knowles (1983: 22) felt that 'There seems to be a prevailing mood in favour of an increased use of children's talk, not only amongst English teachers but across the curriculum generally', more recent classroom research indicates that, notwithstanding a general recognition of the importance of oral work, in practice, a 'rhetoric–reality gap' remains (Mercer 2000). Indeed, Nystrand and Gamoran (1991), in one of the largest studies of classroom discourse ever undertaken, found that while teachers believed that they give prominence to discussion, research did not support this belief. On the contrary, it was discovered that discussion was one of the rarest activities in lessons in English schools – on average less than a minute a day in the classes they studied. The challenge then is twofold: first, to ensure that teachers practise what they preach and regularly include oral work in lessons; and, second, to extend the pupils' learning by not just 'doing' speaking and listening but *teaching* it in a way that leads to the progressive development of ability.

Oral work has two distinct dimensions. It can be the focus of the learning or the frame in which learning occurs. The two are not mutually exclusive, but recognising the difference is important in order to identify how talk can contribute to the whole curriculum and why it has a special place in the English curriculum.

The current appreciation of the importance of talk on the part of English teachers has emerged largely as a result of the work of Andrew Wilkinson (Wilkinson *et al.* 1965), who coined the word 'oracy', and figures such as Britton, Bullock and Barnes. Britton (1972) saw talk as a unique instrument of learning, a view echoed by Bullock (DES 1975), who argued that language has a unique role in developing human learning, while Barnes (Barnes *et al.* 1976) highlighted the importance of 'exploratory talk' as a means of helping children to shape knowledge for themselves.

Speaking, listening and learning

The assertion that children learn through talking is underpinned by the work of Vygotsky and Bruner, who argued that children need to be given the opportunity and time to play with ways of articulating their own ideas and accepting, modifying or rejecting those of others:

> an essential feature of learning is that it creates the zone of proximal development: that is, learning awakens a variety of internal developmental processes that are able to operate only when the child is interacting with people in his environment and in co-operation with his peers.

> (Vygotsky 1978: 90)

Vygotsky's model of learning stresses the need for structured intervention designed to extend the limits of the child's world. Playing with language in a structured way helps pupils to bridge the gap between knowledge 'out there' and the experience through an inner dialogue which results from an external dialogue between the learner and teacher. In order to understand the implications of this, a consideration of the concept of dialogue may be valuable here.

Alexander (2002) probes the nature of classroom talk by drawing a distinction between conversation and dialogue. In a nutshell, his notion is that 'conversation' may be talk that has no appreciable learning outcome, whereas 'dialogue' has the distinct purpose of achieving new understanding. He notes that in the classroom situation dialogue is most usually initiated by the teacher, who is clear about its purpose. However, this purpose is not always clear to the pupils, nor is it often the case that dialogue is initiated by them. As a result, pupils' learning is constrained in two ways. First, when pupils are simply required to respond to questions the teacher poses, they may be inhibited in postulating an answer if they cannot grasp the teacher's frame of reference. Where the teacher has devised a sequence of questions and already formulated the answers the only oral contribution that is valid, in the eyes of the teacher, is the answer that fits the sequence. The result is, at best, stasis, in that the child does not exploit the relationship between thought and language and so neither thought nor language develops. At worst, the result is that the child acquiesces to the teacher's status as someone who knows all the answers and so abdicates from the responsibility of taking any control over their own learning. Second, if pupils do not learn how to initiate dialogue in order to learn about things, their learning will inevitably be limited: 'if we want children to talk to learn – as well as learn to talk – then what they say actually matters more than what teachers say' (Alexander 2002: 8).

The difference between conversation and dialogue may be illustrated by reference to dramatic literature. The dialogue of a play is never just reported conversation, but speech that is crafted in order to explore issues and characters' perceptions of them in order to lead an audience to new insights; it is dialogic. The term 'dialogue' may of course simply be applied to the exchange of words between two or more people. The term 'dialogic', though, as Bakhtin helpfully points out, implies an interplay between, and mutual transformation of, the ideas conveyed by those words as a result of such an exchange (Daniels 2001: 64). What is called for in the classroom situation, therefore, is what might be termed 'dialogic conversation'; that is, conversation that has the overriding objective of playing with ways of articulating ideas and that, by doing so, generates and explores new ones. It is through dialogic conversation that pupils learn how to 'Acknowledge other people's views, justifying or modifying their own views in the light of what others say' (DfEE 2001a: 28).

It is through the act of articulating ideas that those ideas become crystallised. In the National Key Stage 3 Literacy Framework one of the stated objectives for the teaching of speaking and listening is that pupils should be able to 'answer questions pertinently, drawing on relevant evidence or reasons' (DfEE 2001a: 28). However, speaking and listening work that only consists of question and answer style dialogue does not allow room for such play and as a consequence what children learn about the ideas under scrutiny or the way language develops and imparts ideas is atrophied. Instead, children need to be able to 'use exploratory, hypothetical and speculative talk as a way of researching ideas and expanding thinking' (DfEE 2001a: 24).

Speaking and listening across the curriculum

Although the current National Curriculum in England does not make explicit reference to oral work as a means of learning it is implied in the general requirements that teachers: 'use teaching approaches appropriate to different learning styles, use, where appropriate, a range of organisational approaches, such as setting, grouping or individual work, to ensure that learning needs are properly addressed and vary subject content and presentation so that this matches their learning needs'. Moreover, the expectation is that pupils should be taught in all subjects to use language precisely and cogently in their speech and to 'listen to others, and to respond and build on their ideas constructively' (DfEE 1999a: 40). This is further elaborated in the programmes of study for different subjects. For example, in history pupils have to: 'communicate their knowledge and understanding of history, using a range of techniques, including spoken language, structured narratives, substantiated explanations and the use of ICT' (DfEE 1999b: 20). In maths they are required to:

■ interpret, discuss and synthesise information presented in a variety of forms;

- 'communicate mathematically, making use of diagrams and related explanatory text' (DfEE 1999c: 40);
- 'examine critically, and justify, their choice of mathematical presentation of problems involving data' (DfEE 1999c: 53).

Around the same time that the National Curriculum was first being introduced, John Dixon noted that: 'Schools' statements of aims often mentioned the importance of oral communication, but few have reached the stage of developing a policy for implementing such aims' (Dixon 1988: 43). Findings such as this have been echoed more recently by Robin Alexander, who has argued that the value of a more holistic appreciation of the role of language acquisition in learning generally continues to be largely ignored in England (Alexander 2002: 1). The continued privileging of writing over speaking suggests that a full understanding of the relationship between the two uses of language in learning has not yet become manifest in the curriculum or indeed the practice of many teachers. Alexander cites Brice-Heath's assertion that 'there is not a single speech-to-writing continuum, but two continua, the oral and the written, and that they overlap' (Alexander 2002: 2). The distinct differences between speaking and writing as separate modes of communication, and the way they complement each other, need to be understood if children are to be enabled to develop in both continua effectively.

However, simply promoting the use of more discussion in all classrooms may not provide the answer, as Barnes (1988: 52) pointed out:

> I have no doubt that spoken language should play a much greater role in education than it has formerly done, at least in England. But is 'oracy', as it is often conceived, the best way of representing speech in the curriculum? What I have in mind is the possibility that oracy will separate speech as language skills from speech as acting upon the world. Or, to put it differently, I am concerned that oracy will be decontextualised.

The point being made here is that effective spoken language develops through an engagement with live issues and not with 'neutralised pseudo-topics invented solely to give semblance of content to talk for talk's sake'. The purpose of oracy, Barnes argues, should be to learn to understand and influence the world through speech, rather than developing 'decontextualised speech skills'. Barnes's position serves as the basis for some commentary on the way the rationale for the teaching of speaking and listening has developed, for while the roots of oracy lie in the liberal humanist position taken in the 1960s, the National Curriculum grew out of and in many ways still reflects the conservative, traditionalist attitudes of the 1980s. This is implied not only in the apparent privileging of writing over speaking but also in the way achievement in speaking is partially defined by an increasing ability to use standard English; the assumptions being that there is such a thing as standard spoken English, that everyone understands what it is and can recognise it and that being able to use it is altogether a good thing. Such assumptions highlight the value systems that underpin the curriculum and that will, inevitably, impact on the way it is taught.

Speaking, listening and key skills

Further evidence of the functionalist view of education that came to the fore in the 1980s may be identified in the way that the debate surrounding oracy was, in the 1990s, superseded by a concern to address standards of literacy. The cry was to 'get back to the basics' of reading, writing and arithmetic. In such a climate, notions of talk playing an integral part in children's learning held little sway, unless, of course, it was the teacher doing the talking. The swing of the pendulum now, however, appears to be in check as witnessed by this statement in the DfEE's *Year 7 Speaking and Listening Bank*: 'Most definitions of literacy incorporate speaking and listening as an essential ingredient, recognising how talk both supports and feeds on written language, and is an essential aid for learning about and reflecting on language itself' (DfEE 2001a: vi). Similarly, greater attention is afforded to the development of a number of key skills that underpin learning. In her work on teaching in the primary school, Suzi Clipson-Boyles (1998) identifies how practical drama involves acquiring and manipulating a number of these key skills. Her analysis is pertinent to the subject of this book because of the weight she places on speaking and listening as the bedrock for developing the key skills. For example:

- communication (using the spoken and written word along with space, movement and gesture);

- working with others (planning, problem-solving, working collaboratively);

- improving own learning and performance (researching, trialling ideas, evaluating personal contribution to the drama process and performance);

- problem-solving (finding creative solutions to problems, interpreting different stimuli and employing different resources);

- reasoning (considering drama in its context, identifying what needs to be done and how effects will be achieved);

- enquiry (deconstructing images, questioning conventions, researching and experimenting with alternative ways of doing things);

- creative thinking (interpreting character, content and context, designing technical solutions to practical problems);

- evaluation (watching, listening, recognising personal emotional and intellectual responses and using these to inform a consideration of the needs of an audience).

What is of further interest here is the way Clipson-Boyles cites drama as a particularly apposite vehicle for the teaching of these skills.

2

Speaking and listening in English and drama

The English context

THE SUBJECT OF English involves the study of communication through language in its spoken, written and non-verbal forms. In England, the National Curriculum and the Key Stage 3 Literacy strategy objectives state explicitly what pupils should be taught to do under the headings of 'Reading', 'Writing' and 'Speaking and Listening'. When an English teacher selects a resource for a lesson from the seemingly endless supply of fiction and non-fiction available, the central focus is on the language of the material: how it is presented, what it is communicating and how engagement with it will develop further their pupils' understanding of, and ability to use, language expressively.

Learning to speak expressively, though, can seem at odds with the teaching of speaking and listening skills if this is taken to mean inducting children into the use of 'correct' English and Received Pronunciation. Certainly, the National Curriculum charges English teachers with the responsibility to ensure that pupils have the ability to use spoken standard English 'fluently and accurately in informal and formal situations' (DfEE 1999a: 32), and considers it as a variation of language that has importance for national and international communication. Standard spoken English has a particular social and economic value, but it would be misguided to equate the form as being in any way more 'correct' than any other variation. In a side note to the programme of study for speaking and listening (EN 1) examples of non-standard usages are noted:

- subject–verb agreement (they was);

- formation of past tense (have fell, I done);

- formation of negatives (ain't);

- formation of adverbs (come quick);

- use of demonstrative pronouns (them books);

- use of pronouns (me and him went);

- use of prepositions (out the door).

What is apparent here is that a parallel is being drawn with written English, which is standardised by grammatical conventions. In practice drawing such a parallel is problematic. Standard English is a particular form of dialect. Like any other dialect it has its own grammatical structure and vocabulary (Perera 1987: 8). Most children only gain significant experience of a limited number of regional dialects. It would be a rare child, though, who did not regularly experience spoken English in its standardised form, partly because of its use by teachers and largely because of the pervasive nature of the mass media. However, while the use of a standardised form may be accepted in the depersonalised context of a television broadcast, it is not always accepted as the most appropriate form for use at an interpersonal level. Standard English reflects the values of the dominant class and can be an instrument of its power. As such, it illegitimatises other forms that some may consider more 'natural' to them; consider the way the side notes quoted above regard certain grammatical constructions as being 'non-standard' when to many they would seem a perfectly ordinary and satisfactory way of conveying sense in an oral interaction. Consequently, attempting to impose its use could be regarded as a personal affront. In live situations, standard English can also seem considerably less expressive than non-standard forms and therefore less communicative and likely to enhance social interaction. Announcing that 'It is raining heavily outside' may well be economical and grammatically standardised but it doesn't necessarily have the same impact as someone proclaiming 'Why man, it's fair slakin' it doon oot there!'

Much the same argument can be made in comparing regional accents with Received Pronunciation (RP). While dialect refers to vocabulary and grammatical construction, accent is an aspect of pronunciation. RP, while not specific to any region, is an accent nevertheless. The communicative and social value of any given accent is contingent on environmental and social context. As with standard English, children doubtless experience a good deal of RP via television and film. As a result of this extent of exposure, RP, like standard English, may be understood as well in West Kilbride as it is in West Ham. However, a rich Strathclyde accent may be largely incomprehensible to East Londoners simply because they may have had little prior experience of it. This phenomenon cannot be construed as suggesting that RP is any more 'correct' than other accents, for while it may be understood, it won't necessarily be listened to. Accents help to bond people by signalling their regionality and social background but by the same token they can also alienate. What is therefore necessary is that English teachers strive to equip pupils with a repertoire of speaking and listening skills so that they can operate in a wide variety of situations for a range of purposes and in front of different audiences. Furthermore, the value systems attached to different forms of language need to be explored in order to help pupils to ascertain when one form would better express what they wanted than another.

In addition to focusing on the nature of language itself as an object of study, English teachers have, by and large, embraced the idea that children learn through talk and have become adept at using, for example, directed activities related to texts (DARTs) to help pupils to explore the way language expresses meaning. Such activities open up possible interpretations of texts by focusing pupils' attention on the writer's choice of content and form. Similarly, role-play has become a tool adopted by many English teachers as a means of hypothesising and synthesising ideas. It has been noted that discussion arising from work such as this 'accounted for significant gains in students' achievement in literature as measured by tests assessing recall, depth of understanding, and response to aesthetic elements of literature' (DfES 2002d: 31).

However, although teachers believe they give prominence to discussion, observational research does not support this: 'Pupils may have plenty of opportunities for talk but teachers are often unsure what and how to teach' (DfES 2002e: 27). Partly as a result of findings such as these, considerable resources have been employed to generate and disseminate good practice in planning, teaching and assessing speaking and listening as a part of the Key Stage 3 Literacy strategy. What is particularly noteworthy about the materials recently published to support the work of English teachers in this area is not only the variety of engaging individual and group activities designed for use in the English classroom, but also the considerable emphasis the strategy places on drama both as a vehicle for teaching speaking and listening and as a means of furthering pupils' understanding of other aspects of the subject of English. This raises a question about the extent to which drama specialists recognise the role they might play in this aspect of the curriculum.

Speaking and listening in drama

Speaking and listening? Yes, of course. That's all pretty much integral to our work in drama. It's all about communication after all, isn't it?

No. We don't really do anything on speaking and listening. The English department do that stuff.

These two comments represent fairly typical responses from heads of drama when asked about the extent to which programmes of study for English were integrated into their drama curriculum. Such anecdotal evidence seems to indicate that drama teachers somewhat rejoice in not being tied to any nationally enforced programmes of study, yet hold the view that they are in many respects better equipped to teach some aspects of them than their specialist English colleagues. If this is the case, schools may find themselves in something of a double bind. They have teachers with specialist knowledge of oral communication in the drama department but there is no statutory demand that this knowledge is employed. Schools do, however, have a responsibility to ensure that the programmes of study are taught. In the case of speaking and listening it could be that this is sometimes left to English teachers whose real expertise lies elsewhere. A number of questions arise from this. Is it that drama teachers believe that a practical knowledge and understanding of the processes and purposes of oral communication is best acquired through extended contextualised practice rather than as distinct, teachable, skills? If this is the case, how would drama teachers accommodate pupils' work in this area in their assessment of progression in drama, and to what extent could this assessment contribute to the school's duty to record and report on pupils' attainment in the programmes of study? Producing a programme of study involves formulating objectives aimed at ensuring that children acquire knowledge and understanding in such a way that their progress may be assessed. In the case of speaking and listening, the English National Curriculum sought to achieve this by separating out different strands, such as speaking, listening, group discussion and interaction. The overlaps between these strands become apparent when one scrutinises the teaching objectives that need to be met under each heading. This is especially the case in drama, which may be seen as embracing all the other areas. The programme of study as it is delineated seeks to avoid this by focusing on the exploration of dramatic techniques and the scripting, performing and evaluation of plays. In other words, the part played by speaking, listening, discussion and interaction, and the use of standard and other varieties of spoken language, is left implicit in the drama strand whereas it is made explicit elsewhere. For drama teachers this may have two consequences. First, even if they choose to align their curriculum to the programmes of study, they may hold that there is no onus upon them to deal with strands other than the drama strand in any explicit way. Second, the emphasis on scripting and performing plays may lead some drama teachers still beholden to the notion that drama is primarily a learning tool rather than a discrete subject, to reject any adherence to the programme of study completely.

The NFER study *Arts Education in Secondary Schools: Effects and Effectiveness* (Harland 2000: 119–22) recorded these responses regarding the value of drama:

> It makes you sound better . . . nicer . . . how to pronounce things and speak better.

> Say, if you go for an interview, you won't be so shy about it because you've learnt how to speak, project yourself.

Drama has taught me to have a lot more confidence in myself, you know, speaking in front of an audience or speaking in front of . . . not necessarily an audience, but a crowd of people and it's just you speaking.

Here perhaps is another aspect of the double bind in which schools may find themselves. Whether drama teachers think they are teaching speaking skills implicitly, explicitly or not at all, pupils seem to recognise how work completed in drama can be applied to the wider context of effective oral communication. If this really is the case, do they not have a right to have their learning accredited by their drama teachers?

Embedded within these comments lie questions regarding the production of a curriculum for the teaching of speaking and listening that pupils will recognise as providing them with useful knowledge and skills, and to which both English and drama teachers feel able to contribute. Any such coherence must be contingent on finding an acceptable interface between ideology – that is, the fundamental beliefs concerning what constitutes useful skills and knowledge – and pragmatism resulting from the need to fulfil externally imposed requirements. Simply adopting a 'live and let live' position, or alternatively one that 'passes the buck', is unlikely to do the job. What is called for is a reflection on the nature of existing attitudes in English and drama departments and a consideration of how these may need to change in order to tackle the issue in a way that does not compromise the philosophy underlying practice in either English or drama as discrete subjects.

While the NFER study gives a valuable insight into a broad range of aspects of arts education in England, its limitations need to be recognised. Foremost among these is the fact that the study focused primarily on just five case study schools. In pursuit of a greater appreciation of how representative the reported views were, 30 drama teachers involved in the University of Reading Schools Partnership were surveyed through questionnaires and semi-structured interviews regarding their position on the programmes of study for speaking and listening. Twenty-five of the teachers stated that they were aware of the most recent programmes of study and all but one claimed that teaching children to speak and listen effectively constituted a part of their everyday work in drama. However, only two teachers stated that their work in drama was actually informed by the programmes of study.

Table 2.1 charts the teachers' responses to the question of whether they felt they were covering the different strands of the programmes of study explicitly or implicitly. The responses give an insight into drama teachers' attitudes towards and understanding of the national requirements.

At face value, these responses suggest that while drama teachers acknowledge speaking, listening and group discussion as factors in drama, there is a fairly even split between those who set out to teach them as distinct skills, and those who see

TABLE 2.1   Drama teachers' coverage of the EN 1 programme of study

EN 1 programme of study: strands	Dealt with *explicitly* as part of the drama curriculum	Dealt with *implicitly* as part of the drama curriculum
Speaking	15	15
Listening	17	13
Group discussion and interaction	18	12
Drama	25	5
Standard English	3	27
Language variation	8	22

the skills as being subsumed into the broader project of drama education. It is interesting to note that five of the teachers stated that even the specific programme of study for the drama strand was only an *implicit* part of their work. Further investigation of these responses offered different explanations for this, varying from an overall disregard of the National Curriculum *per se* to the more strongly held belief that the drama curriculum involved more than was delineated in the English orders. Most notable here is the response to the notion that the study of standard English and language variation could constitute an explicit part of the drama curriculum. Certainly, there was suspicion of the term 'standard English' and an uncertainty as regards what the teaching of language variation involved. Once again, further questioning revealed that drama teachers still tend to correlate standard English with RP and balked at the idea of teaching this on ideological grounds. Conversely, many admitted to commenting frequently on pupils' diction and clarity, especially when working with scripts, and their use of slang and collo-quialism in improvised work where it was deemed inappropriate to the character. Typically, the drama teachers reported that they tended to ask the pupils them-selves whether or not the use of particular varieties of language suited the character and situation, rather than imposing notions of 'correctness'. The follow-ing comment suggests a view that being more *explicit* about what constitutes language variation is not in fact called for in order to create and perform a piece of drama: 'The thing is that they already know. If I say, for example, "Hmmm, do you think a newsreader would really say that?" then they say "No" and they change it so that it does sound more authentic.' Without further reflection and teacher input such a position falls a long way short of the stated requirements to consider cur-rent influences on spoken language, attitudes towards language use and the development of the language over time.

Over half of the questionnaire respondents said that they considered pupils' progress in speaking and listening to be a part of their general assessment of drama, but only 10 said that their assessment was used as a part of the school's overall assessment of pupils' progress against the programme of study. The reason for this lay in the lack of co-ordination between English and drama departments, with 20 of the respondents saying there was no co-ordination whatsoever. Nevertheless, all the respondents claimed that they were either very able (26) or quite able (4) to teach pupils how to speak and listen for a range of purposes, as set out in the programmes of study. Moreover, an overwhelming majority (28) thought that the teaching of speaking and listening should not be the sole preserve of the English department.

These crude results seem to support the anecdotal evidence that while drama teachers feel they have the ability to deliver the programmes of study, either their expertise is not being used, or they are choosing not to apply it to the formal requirements as they are stated.

Working together

One of the things that emerged from the Reading research was evidence of a rift, and in some cases competition, between English and drama departments, hindering a coherent delivery of the programmes of study:

> Our English department wants drama back in English and therefore any liaison such as communication for the teaching of the drama components of the NC is not really possible. This is a weakness which does not benefit the pupils and I recognise this. However, my main concern is to keep drama as a separate department and as a specialist subject at KS 3. The English department does not accept that drama has its own place in the curriculum other than as part of English.

> After our Ofsted report, one point which was raised was how English and drama as separate departments should collaborate at KS 3 and KS 4 for speaking and listening. There is a reluctance to do this from some staff members as they feel that drama does not and should not be part of the English programmes of study. I feel, however, that there needs to be communication as to how it is being taught in both areas to ensure the requirements are being fulfilled. The head of faculty supports this collaboration but whether anything will materialise from this remains doubtful.

By comparison, there was a willingness among some drama teachers to co-operate and co-ordinate their work with English colleagues. In some cases this relationship is still tentative. In others it has been more firmly established and suggests the development of a praxis that positively embraces an approach to teaching speaking and listening that is built on an understanding of the set requirements and reflection on ideological values regarding the nature and purpose of drama as a curriculum subject. However, such positive moves towards integrating work in drama and English were reported in only a few cases. More typical was the view that while the English orders posed no threat to a discrete curriculum in drama, a lack of communication with the English department was resulting in the delivery of some areas of the programme of study being left to chance:

> Any scheme of work in drama should cover some areas of speaking and listening. For example:
>
> 'Making' – persuasion, argument, exploration: 3a, b, c, 4a, b.
> 'Performing' – adapting language and speech for different audiences (we do a lot of this in Year 9 from adverts to TIE pieces): 1a, c, f, 4a, b, c.
> 'Responding' – 1g, 2e, 3b, 4d.
>
> It seems strange to me also the English and drama departments at this school do not liaise at all regarding which elements of speaking and listening are being covered and by whom. A lot is taken for granted, i.e. drama will deal with area 4 and English will do the rest.

On the question of the assessment, the overriding message from the drama teachers was that the requisite knowledge and skills were integral to the broader project of learning to communicate in the context of making, performing and responding to drama, and it was sufficient to report them as such. Responses indicated that drama teachers may, by and large, have considered the programmes of study for speaking and listening and see themselves as contributing to pupils' progress in the acquisition of at least some of the skills involved.

If the only problem of delivering EN 1 effectively concerned drama and English departments working more closely together this could presumably be remedied by teachers putting aside old grievances and co-ordinating their practice. But is it really as simple as this? Could it be that underpinning current rifts is a lack of mutual understanding as to what the purpose of teaching speaking and listening might be? Could it be that just as drama teachers see their subject as including aspects of the other areas of EN 1, the separate headings of the programme of study suggest a way of looking at the processes of oral communication that results in a confusion regarding the purpose of the programme and effective methods of teaching and assessing it?

The term 'speaking and listening' is perhaps all too often used as a catch-all that, in actuality, gives precedence to the act of speaking and largely assumes that listening will inevitably take place as a consequence. Beyond the physical activity of speaking and listening, though, *communication* is a two-sided process. It involves the transmission of a series of encoded signals, via a given medium, that are then received and decoded. In the specific case of dialogic communication, the receiver must return some kind of a signal in order to acknowledge that the original message has in fact been received and decoded. However, verbal communication is to some extent dependent upon an appreciation of idiom. That is to say that, far from being devoid of grammar, spoken language has a highly complex grammar. For communication to occur, both parties need a considerable appreciation of the way certain grammatical codes are applied in any given situation (the idiom). In the case of oral communication this grammatical complexity is exacerbated by the proliferation of non-verbal signifiers that accompany the words spoken. While some of these are aural – for example, tone, pitch, volume and pace – others are visual.

In answer to the question 'why teach speaking and listening skills', both English and drama teachers tend to focus on interactivity, which is seen as being more valuable and relevant to their pupils' lives than decontextualised formal presentations. The significance of this observation may be that while English teachers need to achieve a better understanding of the part visual signifiers play in effective communication, drama teachers need to reassess their understanding of the relationship between spoken and written grammar and what is actually meant by terms such as 'standard English'. By sharing and discussing their understanding of what is required in the teaching of speaking and listening, and their own views of why and how it might be taught, English and drama teachers may discover a common ground that will allow them to develop a more coherent and thus more effective curriculum. The net result will be that children not only achieve a better practical understanding of what constitutes appropriateness, but are assessed in a way that is more meaningful to them. Such an ideal is clearly not beyond the bounds of possibility, as this response from one of the drama teachers surveyed demonstrates:

> All [drama] Schemes of Work for KS 3 have been written in accordance with the new NC Orders for English. I have worked with the head of English in order to ensure that the requirements for EN 1 are covered and have Schemes of Work that are directly related to the English Schemes of Work.
>
> The increased reference to drama within the English Orders is very encouraging. The aspects of EN 1 that refer specifically to drama are clearly highly compatible with our curriculum as a distinct subject. I believe that a drama department has a lot to offer a separate English department in terms of teaching expertise and practical means of delivering aspects of the speaking and listening requirements. I also feel, however, that a drama curriculum must be broader than the range of skills specified in the English Orders. The practical problem that a drama specialist would have to face, if responsible for assessing, monitoring, recording and reporting on speaking and listening, is one of sheer volume of pupils taught versus curriculum time. This is not to say that a drama department should not be involved. The system we have implemented is:

- The drama department now attends one English meeting per term largely to advise and share good practice in drama education.
- English colleagues have been invited to observe drama lessons to assess their pupils for speaking and listening and learn new skills to make them more comfortable with delivering practical drama.
- We are going to inform the English department of skills taught in the drama schemes of work, identifying when they are taught. Also, we are providing them with lists of skills that pupils should be comfortable using with correct drama terminologies in order that pupils recognise the links between English and drama more readily.

While no specific mention is made here of an existing consensus regarding the purpose of teaching speaking and listening, the impetus at least to start looking at the issue is laudable. If the main purpose of teaching children different functions of language is to enable them to adapt their own speech acts appropriately, English and drama teachers could help their pupils considerably by identifying more precisely the function their own disciplines have in this process.

3

Speaking and listening in the curriculum

Why teach speaking and listening?

WHILE *A Language for Life* (the Bullock Report, DES 1975) proved to be a particularly influential official expression of concern about children's oral work in schools, it was not the first. The Norwood Report (HMSO 1943) stated that no school was doing its duty by the community if it did not do everything in its power to help its pupils to use speech that could be understood in any part of the country.

The focus here is on the socio-economic function of speech: a school's duty is to serve the community and the pupil by ensuring that speech is standardised and easily understood by all. In the context of the time, the inference was that children should be inducted into the use of standard English and RP to the detriment of local dialects and accents. While current concerns with inclusivity and the protection of individual and regional identity would reject such a project, it is difficult to deny that teachers do have a responsibility to ensure that their pupils have sufficient control of spoken English to be able to operate confidently and competently in the vast myriad of spoken situations that their life will present. Although 1943 was a long time ago the following extracts from NFER research in 2000 demonstrate that similar concerns are still extant:

> Teachers talked about language development in terms of clarity of speech and sometimes elocution, and being able to articulate opinions and speak confidently. Pupils too saw these outcomes as particular types of language development, but also talked about having the language to deal with a variety of situations. Thus, transfer to other subject areas and other situations outside of the arts became an important aspect to this effect.
>
> (Harland 2000: 117)

Referring specifically to the role of drama in the development of speaking skills, the NFER reported that: 'The ability to express views and articulate opinions was cited by many of the pupils. Some referred to this as "speaking out", while a few others related it to expressing their own views' (Harland 2000: 119). Pupils also identified the need to enhance their speaking skills for commercial as well as social purposes: 'Say, if you go for an interview, you won't be so shy about it because you've learnt how to speak, project yourself' (Harland 2000: 121). This echoes Kingman, who saw similar reasons for teaching speaking and listening, since 'ability in language can contribute powerfully to adaptability, as a resource for continued education, for the acquisition of new knowledge and skills and for widening the accessible range of jobs' (DES 1988b: 8).

Kingman, however, valued the promotion of oracy beyond the mechanistic by noting the greater social value of speaking and listening in his proclamation that democratic society relies on people having the linguistic ability to discuss, evaluate and make sense of what they are told, in order to take effective action on their own part. If the limits of a person's language are indeed the limits of their world, then furnishing young people with the opportunity to extend their linguistic register becomes a moral imperative. Nevertheless, setting out to *teach* pupils how to speak and listen may imply an 'empty vessel' view of learning in which pupils are filled up to the required level with information on *how* to speak and listen. As pointed out in Chapter 1, and discussed further in Chapter 4, any judgement of how children should speak is dependent on values regarding the social, economic or developmental purpose of talk. Whatever the underlying values, though, explicitly teaching pupils *how* to speak and listen involves children simultaneously using the same skills to enhance their learning *per se*. In this sense there is a close relationship between focusing on *learning to talk* and 'exploratory talk', where the emphasis is on *using* talk to learn. This interrelationship was recognised by Kingman:

> In addition to encouraging the development of speech for communication, teachers need to encourage talk which can be exploratory, tentative, used for thinking through problems, for discussing assigned tasks, and for clarifying thought; talk is not merely social communication, it is also a tool for learning. To say 'merely' is not to dismiss talk that is intended as a performance. Often both kinds of talk emerge from the same activity.

> (DES 1988b: 43)

The relationship between learning to speak and speaking to learn has considerable implications both for the way speaking and listening is addressed in the curriculum and for how it is assessed. Drawing on the work of Vygotsky, as outlined in Chapter 1, many activities promoted recently as effective means of raising levels of thinking and creativity in the classroom involve collaborative group work tasks. The relationship has certainly been given renewed attention in England in recent years. Following reviews of the National Literacy Strategy in Primary Schools, research has suggested that the omission of speaking and listening from the strategy has led to an unbalanced focus on reading and writing, which in turn has had detrimental effects not only on the development of oral communication skills but on cognitive ability. In one study it was found that early gains in cognitive ability were not sustained beyond the age of seven, and children with the best scores at age three were doing worse at five. Anne Locke and Jane Ginsborg attributed their findings to children's limited exposure to spoken language and concluded that more needed to be done to create rich language environments in nursery schools, reception classes and Year 1 if the strategy was to contribute to higher levels of literacy (Ginsborg 2002).

Speaking and listening in the National Curriculum

In England, around a third of the National Curriculum is concerned with the use and development of speaking and listening. This balance is not exclusive to the subject of English. Within each subject area there are clear links made to EN 1 (speaking and listening) in order to recognise the importance of oral work to learning. This is encouraging and in practice should lead to classrooms where talk is used to learn and, in the process of learning, children will learn how to talk. However, it is disappointing that under the section on language across the curriculum only a simple and functional view of speaking and listening is given: 'In speaking, pupils should be taught to use language precisely and cogently. Pupils should be taught to listen to others, and to respond and build on their ideas and views constructively' (DfEE 1999a: 40).

The National Curriculum for English outlines what schools should deliver under the standard headings of 'Knowledge, Skills and Understanding' and 'Breadth of Study'. The first of these sections lists what pupils should be taught under the sub-headings of Speaking, Listening, Group Discussion and Interaction, Drama, Standard English and Language Variation. The second provides the range of activities, contexts and purposes through which the knowledge, skills and understanding should be taught.

For secondary age children (11–16) the National Curriculum (DfEE 1999a: 33) lists the types of talk that should be taught as:

■ describing, narrating, explaining, arguing, persuading, entertaining;

■ extended contributions to talk in different contexts and groups;

■ presentations to different audiences.

While this is obviously not a comprehensive list of the way spoken communication is used, it does offer teachers a basis from which activities can be planned. Similarly, while the list of skills involved in speaking is not exhaustive, at least it embraces the idea that oral communication involves more than the spoken word alone, recognising, for example, the benefit of the following activities:

- use illustrations, evidence and anecdote to enrich and explain their ideas;
- use gesture, tone, pace and rhetorical devices for emphasis;
- use visual aids and images to enhance communication (DfEE 1999a: 31).

While the curriculum for speaking and listening acknowledges 'language variation', the importance of being able to use standard English fluently in different contexts is strongly emphasised:

Pupils should be taught about how language varies, including:

a) the importance of standard English as the language of public communication nationally and often internationally
b) current influences on spoken and written language
c) attitudes to language use
d) the differences between speech and writing
e) the vocabulary and grammar of standard English and dialectal variation
f) the development of English, including changes over time, borrowings from other languages, origins of words, and the impact of electronic communication on written language.

(DfEE 1999a: 32)

Even when placed in the broader perspective of language variation, the concern with standard English remains a contentious issue, in that the term can still imply a preoccupation with ensuring that pupils are taught to talk 'correctly' in the way that Norwood suggested in 1943. Nevertheless, the National Curriculum placed oral work on a par with reading and writing. Subsequent to its introduction, the National Literacy Strategy at Key Stage 3 and rejuvenated GCSE specifications have had considerable influence on what teachers actually deliver in the classroom.

The Key Stage 3 strategy

The National Literacy Strategy (DfEE 1998), which was introduced into primary schools in England in 1998, did not contain a separate element for speaking and listening. As noted above, this may prove to have been a mistake given the importance of oral work to overall cognitive development. While the Key Stage 3 Literacy Strategy, launched in 2001, does contain a specific strand for speaking and listening, the absence of a structured and systematic grounding in speaking and listening skills on which to build constitutes something of a problem for the secondary teacher, suggesting a need for them to establish a baseline for incoming pupils. The Key Stage 3 framework provides a hierarchical list of skills that pupils should be taught during Years 7, 8 and 9 and an array of resources have been produced, which exemplify perceived good practice and direct teachers towards methods that will help pupils to learn the required skills in each year. There is a danger, however, that some teachers could be misled into believing that simply following the recommended activities will lead directly to the acquisition of the prescribed skills without an apposite consideration of the pupils or the whole context of the work being taken into consideration. The reality is that pupils will not learn how to make a speech simply by giving one, or know how to modify and justify a point of view simply by being asked to do it. While they will already have some knowledge and experience of speaking in different contexts and for different purposes, the role of the secondary school teacher is to recognise this and build upon it.

Despite the fact that, on paper, speaking and listening may seem to have the same status as reading and writing, in the curriculum subject of English they can still all too often remain the poor relations to these strands. This is ironic given that so much research points to strong oral skills underpinning achievement in reading and writing.

Speaking and listening at GCSE

At Key Stage 4, speaking and listening constitutes 20 per cent of GCSE English assessment. Although the examination boards provide a variety of specifications for English, allowing for different combinations of coursework and exam papers, the syllabus structure for speaking and listening is the same across all the boards. For example, in the AQA specification (AQA 2002: 13) there are three assessment objectives for speaking and listening:

1 Communicate clearly and imaginatively, structuring and sustaining their talk and adapting it to different situations using standard English appropriately.

2 Participate in discussion by both speaking and listening, judging the nature and purposes of contributions and the roles of participants.

3 Adopt roles and communicate with audiences using a range of techniques.

English teachers are required to submit details of three assessment activities to the examination board: one for individual extended contribution, the second for group interaction and the third for a drama focused activity. In doing so teachers also have to cover three triplets that prescribe the purposes for the talk: (a) explain, describe, narrate; (b) explore, analyse, imagine; and (c) discuss, argue, persuade. Finally, using the assessment criteria provided, the teacher must award an overall mark out of 25 for the work.

This structure mirrors the same triplets that pupils have to master in writing and provides three discrete contexts for the work. The mark contributes to the final GCSE, so it is important that teachers address this part of the course fully. The specifications cover a range of contexts through which a variety of skills may be taught. Teachers carry out assessments throughout the course, submitting the best marks at the end of the year. The model allows for skills to be practised and nurtured and removes from pupils the pressure of a one-off oral test. It also gives teachers the scope to create situations in which pupils can speak freely and confidently.

Set against the flexibility of this model is the pressure of time and the need for English teachers to cover large amounts of literature and non-fiction material in the other parts of the GCSE course. The 60 per cent weighting for the written examination can dominate a teacher's planning. Formal oral assessment can become an inconvenience and reduce the work to something that must be done and recorded, rather than being the foundation upon which other learning is built. However, during the course of study there will be a significant amount of speaking and listening, much of it facilitating the teaching of examination material. Without strategic planning and the careful selection of materials and activities, though, this may neither explicitly teach speaking and listening skills nor develop the pupils' capacity for learning.

Finally, the current requirement that one assessment should be drama based is a double-edged sword. While some English teachers might relish the prospect of doing something more creative and empathetic, there are many who do not feel equipped to do this kind of assessment properly. Here again there may be considerable benefit in encouraging English and drama departments to work together more closely. Some drama teachers will justifiably argue that they are already sufficiently burdened with their own examination work and that it is not their responsibility to do the work of the English department. Resolving the problem may therefore lie in three possibilities. English teachers could seek to develop their ability to teach drama further, or schools could give more support to drama teachers in order to enable them to contribute to this part of the curriculum. Perhaps rather more idealistically, English and drama teachers could be timetabled in such a way as to facilitate some team teaching.

Speaking and listening in the drama curriculum

According to a report by the Secondary Heads Association (1999), approximately half of the secondary schools in the country have a drama department that operates independently from English and just over 60 per cent of the schools surveyed taught drama at Key Stage 3 as a discrete subject. Although drama features as an element of the National Curriculum for English, there are no statutory programmes of study for drama when it is taught as a subject separate from English. This can be a conundrum when it comes to the effective teaching and monitoring of pupils' progress in speaking and listening. On the other hand, when drama and English departments are able to work together in planning to provide pupils with opportunities to extend their knowledge, understanding and skills in this area, the rewards can be considerable. The publication of the Key Stage 3 *Drama Objectives Bank* (DfES 2003) may facilitate such links, providing, as it does, detailed examples of practical activities designed to enhance pupils' knowledge and understanding of drama while raising standards in English. The purpose of each objective is explained and an outline of what to teach in order to address the objective is set out under the headings of making, performing and responding – a framework first developed in the Arts Council of Great Britain's *Drama in Schools* document. Advice is given on how to assess the work undertaken, and performance indicators are offered.

For many drama teachers, identifying 'drama' as something separate from speaking, listening, group discussion and interaction, and indeed standard English and language variation, is mystifying, as all of these may be seen as integral to a subject that seeks to provide young people with opportunities to use language in all its forms to explore and create meaningful experience. This holistic view is recognised in the *Drama Objectives Bank*, which states that:

> Drama is a powerful means and an appropriate context for developing speaking and listening. By being put in formal and informal situations that are outside their everyday experience, by taking a variety of roles and by asking and responding to questions, pupils can employ and evaluate discourses and language registers they would not normally use. Emotional and imaginative engagement underpins the ways pupils seek and create meanings.
>
> (DfES 2003: 4)

While speaking and listening may be seen as representing a third part of the English, a review of the literature quickly reveals that the teaching of speaking and listening skills and knowledge of what oral communication involves is not explicitly afforded the same status in drama education. Two seminal works are worth citing here. In *Drama from 5 to 16* reference is made to the need to relate work in drama to the English National Curriculum, but only two paragraphs refer directly to the development of speaking skills.

> In the course of work in drama, children should be given a variety of experience in four broadly related and interdependent areas. They should:
>
> i.   develop an extensive range of language uses, including many of those referred to in the report of the English Working Group . . .
> ii. learn to move with confidence and purpose . . .

iii. develop the range and flexibility of the human voice and its contribution to creating and sustaining a dramatic impact. This comes about through variations in speed, tone and dynamic control and the ability to articulate with clarity and vitality.

iv. be able to use any available resources to help them communicate dramatically.

(DES 1989: 11)

Drama in Schools, first published by the Arts Council in 1992, proposed a broad programme of study for the subject and again noted drama's inclusion in the curriculum both as a part of English and as a methodology that might be employed across the curriculum. Here again there is scant mention of speaking and listening as any kind of discrete entity with the proposition that 'Pupils should be taught to: Develop voice and movement skills, including mime' being the only direct reference to it at Key Stage 3 (Arts Council of Great Britain 1992: 20).

The study of the spoken word is clearly a major part of the study of the language as a whole in English as a subject. In drama, however, the spoken word is just one element of the polysemic whole of the art form: 'Dramatic meaning cannot lie in words alone, but in voices and the tones of voices, in the pace of speaking and the silences between the gesture and expression of the actor, physical distinctions between him and others' (Styan 1975: 26). Teaching speaking and listening effectively involves setting the spoken word in the context of other aspects of communicative behaviour.

In Chapter 1 it was shown how a number of drama teachers regarded speaking and listening as an implicit part of a curriculum that was more explicitly concerned with making, performing and responding to drama. The original *Drama in Schools* publication was updated in 2003 and the following extract from it illustrates how speaking and listening is seen as a tool to be used rather than an element to be studied independent of any other:

To ensure progression in each key stage pupils should be able to:

- explore and research ideas, issues, plays and other texts such as diary entries, poems, photographs, films and paintings, using a variety of drama skills and techniques
- devise, improvise, shape and structure dramas of different kinds
- use drama skills and knowledge to interpret a range of texts, for example, play scripts, pictures or stories
- prepare and perform both scripted and devised drama for various audiences, using a selection of media
- use and develop their knowledge of drama from different times and cultures, as well as classic and contemporary practice
- reflect on, evaluate and analyse the structure, meaning and impact of their own work and the work of others as both participant and audience

(Arts Council England 2003: 31)

Judith Ackroyd (2001: 12) has noted how some drama educators speak of drama as involving the art of 'making significant' without specifically identifying how 'the articulation of a role is significant in achieving this'. A critique of current GCSE specifications for the subject would seem to support the notion that any propositional knowledge about the nature of spoken English or skill in its use are subservient to a more holistic venture. There are few direct references to the spoken word in the specifications, but what references there are reflect the position of the works discussed above. For example, the Assessment and Qualifications Alliance (AQA) specification requires candidates to 'use appropriate vocal and physical skills, with clarity, fluency, control, appropriateness to character and situation, with pace, projection, vocal and physical flexibility, timing and spatial awareness' (AQA 2000: 16). One of the Oxford, Cambridge and RSA (OCR) Assessment Objectives states that candidates should demonstrate 'Knowledge and understanding of how the language, signs and symbols of theatre are used to communicate dramatic meaning and atmosphere in the range of scripts and their own work' (OCR 2000: 14). For its part, Edexcel defines the drama medium as consisting of:

> The use of costume, masks and/or make up
> The use of sound and/or music
> The use of lighting
> The use of space and/or levels
> The use of set and/or props
> The use of movement, mime and/or gesture
> Use of voice
> Use of spoken language.

(Edexcel 2000: 10)

It is interesting to note that use of voice and spoken language appears at the end of the list and this perhaps indicates a *Zeitgeist* that privileges visual and physical signifiers as modes of communication. However, taking it for granted that pupils will develop an understanding of the spoken word and an ability to speak effectively simply by being involved in drama is unlikely to result in their achieving the best grades for performance work. It may well be that children learn to talk in the first instance through a combination of genetic predisposition and immersion in language as a social mechanism. Nevertheless, relying on osmosis to provide them with the range of speaking and listening skills needed for independent thought in a world economy largely dependent on the skilful use of language is not so much blithe optimism as blatant negligence.

CHAPTER

4

Understanding spoken English

Standard spoken English

ONE OF THE problems teachers face in teaching speaking and listening, in England at any rate, is that the requirements are underpinned by a model of written English whereby pupils' progress is, in part, registered by an increasing ability to use 'standard English' in a range of situations (DfEE 1999d: 55). However, applying the term 'standard English' to speech is highly problematic.

Standard written English may be identified by its use of formulaic codes and conventions that appear to neutralise it by 'establishing a practical consensus between agents or groups of agents having partially or totally different interests' (Bourdieu 1991: 40). Bourdieu argues that any standard written language is determined by and contingent on class and power relationships. The form has to be sustained by a permanent effort of correction on the part of those institutions that depend on it to produce the need for its own services and its own products. An analogy would be the way currency works. The relationship between coins and notes and a bag of apples is dependent upon an agreement between the customer and the vendor based on common practice elsewhere. Why hand over £20 to a stall-holder for a bag of apples when the next door stall only wants 50p? As we know, though, such a relationship is constantly being corrected in line with factors such as inflation and supply and demand. What falls outside the common agreement about this standardised relationship is the possibility that, in payment for a bag of apples, the customer and the vendor strike a bargain that is mutually beneficial to them: one stall-holder may accept the offer to have her car washed, another would prefer to swap the apples for a string of sausages. Both vendor and customer understand the deal because they have agreed relative values between themselves. The standardisation is highly contextualised and rests in a tacit agreement between the two people communicating, even though this arrangement may fall outside institutional standards.

In Bourdieu's analysis the status that is attached to standardised language is imposed rather than socially agreed. While in its written form the use of language may reveal little about its author to the reader, in live spoken interactions the values and prejudices of the listener inevitably play a part in how the discourse is received. Sensitivities about class-based and regional variations in speech are well documented (for example, Labov 1970; Trudgill 1975), as are arguments that teaching 'standard English' is a means of empowering pupils regardless of their social background (Rowe 1975; Bernstein 1990; Honey 1997). Our own research indicates that some teachers still associate the term 'standard English' with 'Received Pronunciation' and reject teaching this on the grounds that it is socially divisive and reinforces the illegitimacy of some modes of speech while privileging others. The research findings of the NFER (Harland 2000), for example, record that the ideologies underpinning drama education remained hotly contested when it comes to a consideration of the subject's role in the teaching of speaking and listening. One teacher, for example, reported that: 'we did a lot of direct speech on "Fair is foul and foul is fair"; you've actually got to get your tongue round that so we can actually do a bit of elocution – almost – and they enjoy doing it.' This teacher's reluctance to state unashamedly that he was dealing with elocution betrays wariness about the implications of the term. The cultural baggage associated with terms such as 'elocution' led another drama teacher in the NFER study to state unequivocally: 'If they say to me it is about elocution, or it is about putting on plays, or it is about facing the front, my answers are definitely no . . . It is about helping kids develop and making sense of the world around them and engaging with it.'

'Elocution' means, literally, the art of speaking expressively. But can the word be used literally when it has so many class-based connotations? While one might wonder how children can engage with their world without attending to what constitutes expressive speech and acquiring a degree of eloquence, historical associations between elocution and standard English, and more particularly the use of RP, may explain teachers' reticence to embrace the term. The conundrum is that both inducting children into the use of standardised language and rejecting it on the grounds that it is a socially divisive imposition effectively maintains the status quo anyway. However, both positions may be undermined by questioning the relationship between language in its standard written form and what is actually accepted as standard in its spoken form.

Language is a form of currency. Put simply, without language you don't get what you want or need. In the social context the value of language is, like any other type of currency, in a constant state of flux. For the most part, written language derives from common spoken usage but selectively legitimised by grammatical rules in the way suggested by Bourdieu. O'Rourke and O'Rourke

(1990: 270) argue that English spellings, for example, are notoriously inconsistent because the movement of sound changes in speech clashes with a class-based imperative to standardise the system. Spellings that once represented sounds reasonably accurately become fixed, while the sounds in common usage move on. If this is the case, any attempt to fix and regulate a standard spoken language for eternity must be doomed to failure. Research into Shakespeare's use of language, for example, suggests that the sound of his speech would be something like a mix between an Irish brogue and a west country drawl. In fact, as the theatre company Northern Broadside amply demonstrate, playing Shakespeare with rich contemporary north of England accents brings his work to life and clarifies the language extremely well. Nevertheless, the changeable nature of language is disturbing to many people, who variously fear it is symptomatic of moral decline and the erosion of traditional social standards.

While arguments regarding the standardisation of written English are largely academic, arguments regarding the nature of standard spoken English and the desirability of teaching young people to use it are largely political. This was never more evident than in the Thatcher government's cessation of the National Oracy Project, which tended towards the conclusion that standard spoken English may be more to do with what is routinely said in different contexts rather than with how it *ought* to be said. However, teaching pupils about the *concept* of standard spoken English alongside notions of language variation might be an altogether more acceptable and productive venture. In the first instance this might involve getting the children to consider their understanding of the term and what values and prejudices their understanding reveals.

Active investigation

While news reporters may commonly be held to model standard spoken English, the considerable variation in their work can be used to reveal the slipperiness of the concept and changing attitudes to spoken language. Ask pupils to compare recorded extracts of the following:

- BBC newsreaders with Channel 4 newsreaders;

- contemporary news programmes and news programmes from the past 40 years;

- news bulletins on BBC Radio 4 and local commercial radio stations.

Ask pupils to identify which broadcasts they thought used standard English and why they thought this.

Point out to the pupils that it is most likely that in each case the broadcaster would have been reading the bulletin from a script. This raises the question of how they may have been equating standard spoken English to accent, including RP, and dialect.

The investigation into the changing nature of standard spoken English can be extended by reviewing extracts of children's television programmes. It is possible to obtain videos and tape recordings of children's TV programmes from the 1960s and 1970s, such as *Andy Pandy*, *Jackanory*, *Watch with Mother* and *Bill and Ben*. Some of these have been remade in recent years, making comparison possible. After watching these programmes pupils are asked to consider:

- What they noticed about the way the presenters speak.

- How they personally responded to the presenters.

- What they thought the presenters felt about the children they are speaking to.

- How they could tell this from the way they were speaking.

What is of the greatest importance is that children consider their own use of language and inspect the values attached to it. Role play can be an effective way of initiating this. For example, tell the class that a pupil has caused an accident by swinging his bag over his shoulder then, turning round to speak to his friend, knocking over a teacher, sending the teacher and her books down the stairs. Ask the pupils to act out the following conversations:

- the pupil to his friend in the playground;

- the pupil when called to explain himself in the headteacher's office;

- the pupil explaining the incident to his parents later that evening.

This activity will demonstrate pupils' implicit understanding of the need to vary their speech in different circumstances. What needs to be discussed is how and when the pupils felt they were using standard spoken English.

Language variation

O'Rourke and O'Rourke (1990: 275–6) note that 'Language both reflects social change and is the instrument of that change . . . We recognise a generation by its characteristic expressions: *ripping*, *smashing*, *fab*, *magic*, and so on. Words change from "plus" words to "minus" words, depending on the values of the time.' We are confronted daily with evidence of the way language moves on and pupils themselves will usually happily supply examples of words they use that seem to be outside the register of most adults. Carter and Adolphs (2003: 13) suggest that 'Some may argue that such a discourse underlines the irreversible decline of standard English into a series of mutually unintelligible sub-languages; another way of seeing such exchanges is, however, to observe the richness and invention of which everyday users of English are capable and to praise the creative invention which results from the mixing.'

Notwithstanding the institutional will to standardise language, modern technology has proliferated new opportunities for people, and perhaps especially young people, to appropriate and indeed invent language that gives expression to their feelings of friendship, intimacy and involvement with each other. For the purposes of daily intimate exchanges, standard English has no value for many; therefore, new modes of speaking and writing are invented and developed. The Internet and the mobile telephone have had a remarkable impact on the amount of communication that takes place among those who would previously have had little or no contact with each other. An intriguing dimension of this new network is the germination of new language varieties. Chat rooms and text messaging have the immediacy and informality of speech, yet, by necessity, require notation. The resultant mutation of written and spoken forms is characterised by the use of a number of devices that exclude those not in the social network in much the same way that spoken modes such as 'thieves' cant' have always done. Bourdieu argues that spoken language forms such as cant are not simply a rejection of dominant modes of speech but speech that is 'adeptly tailored to the markets for which they are produced' (Bourdieu 1991: 22). While being adept at using abbreviations and codes for their own purposes, teenagers are generally unlikely to employ text message shortcuts in other forms of writing, understanding that to do so would be to fail to communicate effectively in any market other than that of the world of fast messaging. Having said that, there have been well publicised instances of examination candidates deliberately choosing to employ such a format and being penalised for doing so. One wonders how examiners might have reacted to Antony Burgess's *A Clockwork Orange* or Russell Hoban's *Ridley Walker*, given these writers' imaginative attempts to capture on paper new variations of the language. Certainly, Bourdieu's critique of *institution* is a helpful tool for understanding the implications of such events. He notes, for example, that an institution 'endows individuals with power, status and resources of various kinds'. The institution endows the speaker with the authority to speak and be recognised by others that speaking in such a way is acceptable (Bourdieu 1991: 8). In the case of text messaging, it is not just 'knowing' the language that gives authority, but contributing to its development by creating new shortcuts that are understood and appreciated by others in the social network, such as in this lively exchange between two teenage girls:

a u jst gt my pics bak! v funi lts of drunknes :s wl brng em in 2skl 2m, owsu? gt dance now gtg mwa xXx

(Hey you, just got my pictures back! Very funny, lots of drunkness [icon of drunken face] will bring them into school tomorrow. How are you? Got dance now, got to go [kiss sound] xXx)

ocool! ilav2 gt min dun2 asap, deyl b alaf! cnt w8 4easta hols now god i rily nida bloke- we r goin onda pul my friend!! lulas ttul x

(Oh cool! I'll have to get mine done too as soon as possible, they'll be a laugh! Can't wait for the Easter holidays now. God, I really need a bloke – we are going on the pull my friend!! Love you like a sister. Talk to you later. X)

Of particular interest here is the incorporation in text message form of both aural and visual signs: the kiss sound and the iconic drunken face. On the face of it, though, the kind of linguistic currency being exchanged by the young through messaging technology may not seem immediately transferable to that other form of 'on-line' communication, live oral interaction (Kempe 2003: 67–8). However, messaging may be regarded as a special form of written speech and is worthy of study on account of it representing a language variation. Similarly, dramatic dialogue, as we shall see, represents another valuable resource for studying the changing relationship between written and spoken English. It is pertinent at this point to consider what we mean by varieties of language. For example:

Literary English	*Hybrid forms*	*Spoken English*
Prose	Dramatic dialogue	Conversation
Poetry	Text messaging	Narration
	Transcription	Formal speech
		Recitation
		'Written speech'

Not wishing here to get bogged down with fine distinctions, what is being suggested is that *prose* could be taken to include fictional narratives, letters, journals and newspaper reports. A distinction could be made between these forms and *poetry*, where the condensed nature of the imagery or use of formal conventions set it aside. By *literary English* we mean anything that is written primarily to be read.

Plays contain elements of literary English in different ways. Clearly, plays can be viewed as pieces of literature but they are most often written for different types of audiences. The ultimate audience is the one that will watch or listen to the play. The details of stage directions are of no immediate consequence to them in that they are aware of the consequences of the directions rather than the written directions themselves. For directors, designers and technicians, though, stage directions have a different value. Conversely, while *dramatic dialogue* is experienced in its written form by those reading the script, the theatre audience experiences it not as literary English but as spoken English. *Transcription* works the other way around, in that it starts as spoken English and is then committed to print. In the cases of both transcription and dramatic dialogue, what is actually written does not represent the whole of what is communicated, given the impossibility of capturing precisely either the vocal qualities that attend what is said or the visual signifiers that accompany speech.

Varieties of spoken English range from casual conversation through organised debate to formal presentation. Spoken English would also include the recitation of literary English, from reading a sermon to reading a news bulletin, and narration, which in itself could be seen to include storytelling, giving instructions, explaining and so forth.

It may be helpful here to review Vygotsky's distinction between oral and written speech and the parallels he draws in them to the difference between monologue and dialogue. Written speech, he notes, 'relies on the formal meanings of words and requires a much greater number of words than oral speech to convey the same idea' (Vygotsky 1962: 142). In the absence of tone of voice and knowledge of the subject we are obliged to use more words and to use them more exactly. This requires planning, even when 'we do not actually write out a draft'. In this sense it may be seen that the cognitive processes involved in writing something down are also utilised in a formal oral presentation, where the speaker is relying on mental preparation to predetermine what he or she intends to say. In some circumstances these processes are also apparent in conversational and discursive speech, where speakers have thought carefully about exactly what they want to communicate in advance (such as when you go to the headteacher to put forward your case for promotion but predict the arguments he will put up in response).

Oral speech, by contrast, presupposes sufficient knowledge on the part of each communicant to permit abbreviations:

> Dialogue implies immediate unpremeditated utterance. It consists of replies, repartee; it is a chain of reactions . . . a word acquires its sense from the context in which it appears; in different contexts, it changes its sense. Meaning remains stable throughout the changing of sense. The dictionary meaning of a word is no more than a stone in the edifice of sense, no more than a potentiality that finds diversified realization in speech.
>
> (Vygotsky 1962: 146)

Notions of what constitutes standard spoken English could derive from a recognition of written speech in its oral form. In other words, speech that appears to be planned and to use words with exactness more closely mirrors language as it is standardised in its written form than spontaneous oral speech. Certainly, it is in this domain that some people, being ill equipped to adapt their speech appropriately to different contexts, find themselves limited in the extent to which their speech acts are regarded as legitimate. However, the reality is that in its oral form written speech is contextualised by the visual and aural signifiers that accompany it, as a result of which the sense of what is being said is changed in ways that do not apply to literary forms of language. The most successful formal speakers are those who, while preparing what they wish to say, also consider and mentally rehearse how they intend to speak in order to make their talk more engaging. In this sense spoken language cannot be completely standardised because the context of live communication is never neutral. It is only by attending to the part aural and visual signifiers play in oral communication that a credible and effective means of both understanding and developing effective speaking skills can be achieved. Indeed, it is clearly the case that the effective use of such signifiers can more than adequately compensate for dialectical variation and other forms of spoken English commonly regarded as 'non-standard'.

Active investigation

Following on the practical exercise suggested on page 30, ask the class to consider the following scenario.

A pupil has slept through the alarm clock going off. In their panic to get to school without being too late they have forgotten to pack their homework and pick up their bus fare. As a result they have arrived very late (they had to walk to school) and been reprimanded by a teacher.

In role the pupils:

- construct a text message to a friend recounting what happened;

- tell a friend about the morning's events at lunchtime;

- explain what happened to a parent;

- mentally prepare and orally deliver an apology to the teacher.

Ask the pupils to discuss how they used language differently in each case. Most particularly, ask them to consider the effectiveness of their use of language in each case in terms of communicating what they wanted to say to the different audiences. This sort of exercise can be used to raise the question of when speech is planned and when it is spontaneous. It also raises the question of what sort of speech is most appropriate to a given circumstance.

Appropriateness

Appropriate is perhaps the most problematic concept that teachers must address in the teaching of speaking and listening, along with the phrase that frequent attends it, *for a range of purposes*. For example, in the National Curriculum for English, the level descriptor for exceptional performance states that 'Pupils select and use structures, styles and registers appropriately in a range of contexts, varying their vocabulary and expression confidently for a range of purposes' (DfEE 1999d).

What is characterised here is a view of spoken English that is essentially functional. If, as posited above, standard spoken English is equated with written speech, where sense is dependent on the words alone, the question must be: to what extent does an explicit knowledge of grammar help pupils to speak 'appropriately' when oral communication is not in fact dependent on the words alone? The standardisation of grammar as it is manifest in written language attempts to make it applicable to the widest possible unseeing, unhearing audience. Oral speech, though, is heard and is most usually seen happening. The words are accompanied by a raft of aural and visual signifiers that can be used to clarify the sense of what is being said. This phenomenon raises a question about the appropriateness of applying the conventions of written grammar to speech and suggests a need to consider further what might constitute 'spoken grammar'.

Understanding the different functions of speech is neither beyond secondary aged children nor fruitless for them. Caroline Coffin (2001: 11) has argued that children arrive in school with considerable grammatical resources already in place; the teacher's objective is then to provide opportunities for them to marshal those resources in an increasing variety of contexts in which both their function and effect are apparent and may be reflected upon.

Speech acts resist standardisation for many reasons. In fact, attempting to apply the rules of grammar to speech in some circumstances can obfuscate meaning and sound clumsy if not ridiculous. A witty example of the stultifying effect on speech of such formalisation occurs in Peter Nichols's play *Forget-Me-Not Lane* when Charles, a father with unrewarded social pretensions, is taken to task on his attempt to speak 'correctly' by his grammar school educated son:

Charles: What a way to dress!
Young Frank: What about *you*! What's your trouser rolled up for?
Charles: For what is your trouser rolled up? (*He pauses. He realises this is not quite right yet.*)
Young Frank: (*smiles*) Up for what is your trouser rolled?
Charles: Don't talk big, you make yourself look small.

The point is that we habitually accept things in speech that are not always acceptable in writing. Attempts to sustain a programme of correcting speech in order to standardise it may lead not only to alienation, loss of self-esteem and resentment against the institution seeking to impose such 'norms', but also to ineffective communication.

A problem with teaching speaking skills lies in the fact that 'We don't have a developed way of talking about talk. Teachers may focus on vocabulary but that is not all we need to know if we are trying to encourage children to be clear, expressive and fluent' (Horner 2002). So, while the National Curriculum moves pupils towards being able to 'maintain and develop their talk purposefully in a range of contexts [and] structure what they say clearly, using apt vocabulary and appropriate intonation and emphasis' (DfEE 1999d: 55), we must ask: to what extent might an understanding of the grammatical features of spoken English, and how they differ from the grammar of written English, help pupils to achieve this?

5

Investigating speech

The features of spoken English

CARTER (2002) HAS argued that the more people know about the forms and structures underlying the processes involved in effective oral communication, the more they will be able to resist formulaic and routinised talk. An explicit inspection of spoken English may contribute to a greater understanding of how habitus – that is, the dispositions that regularly incline us to act and react in the way we do but are not governed by any set rules – affects spoken communication. The purpose of nurturing such an understanding would be to help to extend institutional notions of what constitute legitimate speech acts. This would affect the means by which speaking skills are assessed, and directly contribute to the development of students' confident use of language for a range of purposes.

Carter has identified a number of key features of spoken language that distinguish it from standardised written forms. One way of understanding what these features are and how they work would be to sample 'live' speech. Indeed, Carter's work with CANCODE (Cambridge and Nottingham Corpus of Discourse in English) is aimed at quantitative and qualitative investigation of a range of different speech genres, with an emphasis on recordings and transcriptions of everyday speech. What is offered here is an alternative approach that considers how playwrights have used their observations of live speech acts to create dialogue that, while crafted to serve dramatic functions, nevertheless 'sounds' authentic owing to the way in which some of these features are employed.

Ellipsis

Ellipsis is recognised by the omission of subjects from an utterance on the assumption that the listener knows what is being referred to. For example:

A: [**Would you like to**] Get together tonight?
B: [**That**] Sounds good.
A: [**I've got**] Loads to tell you.
B: About the holiday?
A: [**I had a**] Smashing time.

Examples of ellipsis are as common in dramatic dialogue as they are in real speech. The reason for this is, of course, that abbreviation is compensated for by the aural and visual signifiers present in any 'live' situation. For example:

Varya: Uncle, dear!
Anya: Uncle, you're doing it again!
Gayev: Silence. I say no more.
Lyubov: What was that?
Lopakhin: I don't know. Perhaps a cable in a mineshaft breaking . . . whatever it was it was a long way off.
Gayev: Might have been a bird. A heron perhaps.
Trofimov: Or an owl.
Lyubov: Eerie . . .

In this extract from *The Cherry Orchard* note how a number of references are being made to the situation without recourse to identifying them through explicit speech. Varya's line, 'Uncle, dear!', with its all important exclamation mark, tells us that she is gently urging Gayev to stop whatever it is he's been doing (in this case, rambling philosophically). 'What was that?' and the reply 'I don't know' only make sense when the intervening stage direction is included: the sound of a string breaking. Gayev's familiarity with his companions is suggested by 'Might have been a bird' rather than the more grammatically correct 'It might have been a bird'. Trofimov's reply 'Or an owl' is cognate with the failing light; a theatre audience would of course have the lighting and setting to show that the group are having a picnic and that dusk is falling. The line also has a poetic value: the early appearance of the night bird is a metaphor, in that it suggests an ominence that is picked up by Lyubov's elliptical 'Eerie'.

Active investigation

Ask the class what sort of situations they can think of when it isn't absolutely necessary to state explicitly what you mean. Point out that ellipsis could be used to avoid saying things that are already obvious or may be taboo. For example:

In pairs, pupils improvise a short conversation about something they are both involved in such as a football match. However, they must not say exactly what they are doing but they must make their attitude towards what they are about as clear as possible. For example:

1: So [**what do you think**]?

2: [**I**] Reckon you need to go more [**to the**] right [**hand side of the field**].

1: [**Their defender is a**] Big bloke though. [**Getting past him might be**] Tricky.

2: Try crossing [**the ball**].

Talk about what other visual signals were used to make the attitude clear.

By way of contrast, ask the pupils to work in groups and imagine that one of them has been to see a friend who is very ill in hospital. Once again, the constraint is not to state exactly what the situation is but to convey a shared concern. For example:

1: [**I have**] Been to see him this morning. [**Things are**] Not too good, I'm afraid.

2: Is it what they . . . [**thought**]?

1: [**It's**] Worse. Doctor's saying perhaps just a few weeks [**until he dies**].

2: [**That's**] Terrible. [**Is it**] Definite [**that he will die**]?

1: [**They're going to**] Operate tomorrow. Have a look [**and see if there is anything they can do**].

Once again, talk about the use of visual signifiers and also why, in some situations, people deliberately choose not to be explicit.

Spoken clauses

The extract from *The Cherry Orchard* also provides examples of *spoken clauses*; that is, utterances that stand alone yet contain no verb. 'Or an owl' is one, 'Eerie' is another. In speech, such clauses are often subordinate in nature and used to reinforce or highlight something, as exemplified in this extract from David Storey's play *Home*:

Jack: I say. That was a shock.

Harry: Yesterday . . .?

Jack: Bolt from the blue, and no mistake.

Harry: I'd been half-prepared – even then.

Jack: Still: a shock.

Harry: Absolutely.

In live oral communication such clauses tend to be accompanied by strong visual and aural signifiers, such as a gesture, a facial expression and more particularly the employment of a particular tone of voice. Spoken English is also characterised by clause chains; that is, utterances that, if committed to writing, would be punctuated as sentences, though once again they would contrast strongly with literary prose. Consider, for example, this extract from Arnold Wesker's *Chips with Everything*:

Smiler: LEAVE ME ALONE! Damn your mouths and hell on your stripes – leave me alone: Mad they are, they're mad they are, they're raving lunatics they are. CUT IT! STUFF IT! Shoot your load on someone else, take it out on someone else, why do you want to pick on me, you lunatics, you bloody apes, you're nothing more than bloody apes, so damn your mouths and hell on your stripes! Ahhhhh – they'd kill me if they had the chance. They think they own you, think that anyone who's dressed in blue is theirs to muck about, degrade. YOU BLOODY APES, YOU WON'T DEGRADE ME! Oh my legs – I'm going home. I'll get a lift and scarper home. I'll go to France, I'll get away.

Discourse markers

Discourse markers are used to mark boundaries in spoken communication to signal transitions from one section of what is being said to another. Anyway, okay, well, right and so are common examples. Their use reveals a great deal about what we actually accept as standard spoken English regardless of its difference from formal written English. Consider, for example, this transcript of a teacher talking about her lesson and note how she uses connectives such as *and* and *but* as well as *so* and *because* to signal that she has more to say:

> **Um** . . . it's a difficult lesson because you spend so much time at the beginning of it sitting down sorting out the admin side of stuff which is a pain **but** it has to be done **so** you're always very conscious that when they're sitting down for so long they get restless **and** particularly kids like Robin who's quite a lively child – doesn't have ADHE **but** seems to show symptoms of it **but** is actually a very nice kid **but** a bit disorganised and all over the shop . . . **um** I'm always really anxious in the back of my mind **so** I try and make it as interesting as possible by making sure I keep the pace going and for those who are struggling . . . 'cos I hate doing it **because** there are those children like the girl who came up at the end **um** . . . Amy – who is very dyslexic **and** I know she has problems **but** unfortunately I have to get through it **so** I just look round and say you know . . . **so** I was quite pleased with myself **because** I went so much slower **so** I could actually walk round and see who was struggling **so** I could just immediately say don't stress about it, come at the end of the lesson and do it and then **so** I'll just talk to her – I'm going to write it up and stick it in her book.

This speech is in itself another example of a clause chain. Among its 231 words there are 20 discourse markers, including the use of stabilising sounds such as 'um', which signal that the speaker hasn't yet finished what she has to say. In formal written English one would expect a more refined use of connectives, but in dramatic dialogue we see a hybrid between the two forms. The insertion of discourse markers can help dramatic characters to seem authentic. Playwrights sometimes suggest character traits by incorporating stabilising sounds such as 'er' or 'um' in the dialogue, but more often these sorts of markers are added by the actor interpreting a part. This in itself could be seen as further evidence of the implicit understanding playwrights and actors have of the difference in function and nature between written and spoken English. In the case of both fictional and real characters, though, the overuse of discourse markers, especially stabilising sounds, impedes the economy and impact of what is being said. We all doubtless know how frustrating it is to have to listen to someone 'umming' and 'erring' away or adding interminable conditions to what they are trying to say rather than just spitting it out. However, clause chains and associated discourse markers do not necessarily represent 'sloppy' speech or denote regional, educational or class background (it is worth noting that the teacher quoted above spoke with what would be described as a polished form of RP). Instead, markers and clauses indicate the intricate relationship between thought and oral speech in which ideas are formulated and shaped through the very process of speaking. It may be, however, that they are not as effective a means of emphasising particular points as a more 'writerly' approach. Consider, for example, this lengthy clause chain from Yasmina Reza's play *Art*, which sounds convincingly authentic when it is delivered, yet actually carries far fewer discourse markers than one would expect in a transcription of genuine spontaneous talk:

> Catherine adores her step-mother, who more or less brought her up, she wants her name on the invitation, she wants it and her step-mother is not anticipating, **which** is understandable, since the mother is dead, not appearing next to Catherine's father, **whereas** my step-mother, whom I detest, it's out of the question her name should appear on the invitation, **but** my father won't have his name on it if hers isn't, unless Catherine's step-mother's is left off, **which** is completely unacceptable, I suggested none of the parents' names should be on it, after all we're not adolescents, we can announce our wedding and invite people ourselves, **so** Catherine screamed her head off, arguing that would be a slap in the face for her parents who were paying through the nose for the reception, and particularly for her step-mother, who's gone to so much trouble when she isn't even her daughter **and** I finally let myself be persuaded, totally against my better judgement, **because** she wore me down, I finally agreed that my step-mother, whom I detest, who's a complete bitch, will have her name on the invitation, **so** I telephoned my mother to warn her, mother, I said, I've done everything I can to avoid this, **but** we have absolutely no choice, Yvonne's name has to be on the invitation, she said, if Yvonne's name is on the invitation, take mine off it . . .

The whole of this speech consists of a 900-word-long 'sentence' heavily punctuated by commas, yet, as one can see in this section of comparable length to the earlier transcription (233 words), it contains far fewer discourse markers (9) than one might expect in 'real' talk.

A major feature of oral communication is that discourse markers are not exclusively verbal. In any analysis of improvised or text-based performance, drawing attention to the way in which gestures and facial expression signal that the speaker has more to say, or is positioning his audience emotionally, reinforces the argument that any grammatical analysis of the spoken word that omits other signifiers is not only impoverished but palpably misleading.

Active investigation

Make a tape recording of two contrasting radio interviews; for example, one from a local radio phone-in show and another from Radio 4's *Woman's Hour*. Play the recordings and simply ask the pupils to make a tally chart of the number of discourse markers they detect in two columns:

Stabilisers (er, um, ah, you know etc.) *Connectives (and, but, so etc.)*

Recording 1

Recording 2

Discuss the effect the use of these discourse markers has on the listener. What do they suggest about the speaker? What does their use tell us about the context in which they are speaking? It is also worth considering, in comparing recordings in this way, whether there seems to be any correlation between accent and dialect (including RP) and the frequency of stabilisers and connectives. What such a study can reveal is that while RP can often be interpreted as being standard English, its speakers do not necessarily apply the grammar of written English to their talk any more than anyone else.

Modality

'In most standard written grammars *modality* is described mainly in terms of modal verbs (e.g. may, might, can, could, should, ought to)' (Carter 2002: 7). In spoken communication modal expressions, like discourse markers, may also include looks, gestures and sounds. Tone of voice is a major factor in modality, as is the way words are placed in the overall utterance. Modality plays an enormous part in successful communication because it is an essential means of negotiating relationships and positioning one's audience. Modality is used by skilful speakers to 'soften' the impact of what is being said when people are persuading or asking for something. Speech that lacks modality can impede the development of productive relationships. For example, compare the way Mrs Kay and Mr Briggs go about forming, or failing to form, productive relationships in these two extracts from Willy Russell's *Our Day Out*. In the first extract, notice the way Mrs Kay uses syntax and the Driver's name to establish a productive relationship. Notice also how she deliberately times her movements in order to effectively control his emotional response. Instances of modality, both verbal and visual, are in bold.

Mrs Kay: Can I have a word with you, **driver**, in private?

The DRIVER *comes off the coach.* **She manoeuvres it** *so that the* DRIVER *has his back to the* KIDS *and other* TEACHERS.

What's your name, **driver**?

Driver: Me name? I don't usually have to give me name.

Mrs Kay: **Oh come on**. What's your name?

Driver: Schofield, Ronnie Schofield.

Mrs Kay: Well, **Ronnie**. (*She points.*) Just take a look at those streets.

He does so and as he does she motions, behind his back, indicating that the other TEACHERS should get the KIDS onto the coach.

Ronnie, would you say they were the sort of streets that housed prosperous parents?

Driver: We usually do the better schools.

Mrs Kay: All right, **you** don't like these kids, **I** can see that. But do **you** really have to cause them so much pain?

Driver: What have I said? I only told them to wait.

Mrs Kay: **Ronnie**, the kids with me today don't know what it is to *look* at a bar of chocolate. Lemonade **Ronnie**? Lemonade never touches their lips. (*We should almost hear the violins.*) These are the children, **Ronnie**, that stand outside shop windows in the pouring rain, looking and longing, but never getting. Even at Christmas time, when **your** kids from the better schools are singing carols, opening presents, **these** kids are left, **outside**, left to wander the cold cruel streets.

RONNIE is grief stricken.

Behind him, in the coach, the KIDS are stuffing themselves stupid with sweets, chocolate and lemonade.

MRS KAY leaves RONNIE to it and climbs on board. As RONNIE turns to board the coach all evidence of sweets and lemonade immediately disappears. RONNIE puts his hand in his pocket, produces a few quid.

Driver: (*to the KID on the front seat*) Here y'are son, run to the shops an' see what sweets y'can get with that.

Now consider how Mr Briggs fails to strike a productive relationship in this extract. Here again names and pronouns are used to establish a mode but in this instance the effect is wholly negative. Movements and gestures in this instance are reactive rather than contrived and so accentuate the deepening rift between the characters. A useful exercise is to ask pupils to rehearse contrasting extracts such as these and then reflect on how tone of voice, facial expressions, gesture, movement and the proximity of the characters both generate and convey their relationship. Here again, key words that signal modality are emboldened:

Briggs: **Carol Chandler**, just come here. Who gave **you** permission to come on these cliffs?

Carol: (*moving to the edge*) No one.

She turns and dismisses him.

Briggs: **I'm** talking to **you Miss Chandler**.

She continues to ignore his presence.

> Now just **you** listen here **young lady** . . .

Carol: (*suddenly turning*) Don't **you** come near me!

Briggs: (*taken aback by her vehemence, he stops*) Pardon?

Carol: **I** don't want **you** to come near me.

Briggs: Well in that case just get yourself moving and let's get down to the beach.

Carol: **You** go. *I'm* not comin'.

Briggs: **You** what?

Carol: Tell Mrs Kay she can go home without me. **I'm** stoppin' here, by the sea.

Pause.

Briggs: Now just **you** listen to me. I've had just about enough today, just about enough and I'm not putting up with a pile of silliness from the likes of **you**. Now come on!

He starts towards her but she moves to the very edge of the cliff.

Carol: Try an' get me an' I'll jump over.

BRIGGS *stops in his tracks, astounded and angered.*

Briggs: (*shouting*) Listen **you stupid girl**, get yourself over here this minute.

She ignores him.

Active investigation

Ask the pupils to imagine that they have been stopped by a stranger asking directions. They are only partly sure how to direct the stranger to their destination but wish to be as polite and helpful as possible. The conversation might go something like this:

1: **Excuse me, young lady**, could you tell me **please** how to get to the Hilton Hotel?
2: **I think** you need to go straight on then **try** taking the first right. Then you'll see a roundabout and **hopefully** you'll see it signposted.
1: **Thank you. Do you know, by any chance**, how far it is, **about**?
2: **I'd say it was probably about** two miles, **but I'm not really sure**.
1: **Now**, I need the Hilton North rather than the Central one. **Will that be the right one do you think?**
2: **I'm sorry, I really couldn't say for certain.** I don't know which is which.

Ask the pupils to try to improvise the conversation again without using any modal expressions. As far as possible they should try to avoid using any gestures and remain straight-faced. For example:

1: Tell me how to get to the Hilton Hotel.
2: Straight on. First right then left at the roundabout.

1: How far is it?

2: Two miles.

1: I want the Hilton North not the Central one.

2: I don't know which is which.

Discuss the different effects created by each improvised conversation. How do listeners respond when they are spoken to directly by speakers who do not use modal expressions? How does it feel either speaking without gesturing or listening to someone who uses no gestures?

Deixis

Deixis is a feature of written and spoken language that orientates the listener or reader by drawing their attention to particular features of a situation. There are only around twenty words, such as this, that, there, here, that serve this function but they occur much more in speech than in writing because they are commonly linked to visual or aural signs. Like ellipsis, deictical utterances assume a shared knowledge. For example: 'Look at that! Who put it there? Help me move this over to hide it.' As with other features of spoken language, deictical utterances are likely to be accompanied not only by gestures but by the employment of variations in tone and volume that accentuate meaning. In dramatic dialogue, deictical words may often be considered to function as intra-dialogic stage directions; that is, the vocabulary itself suggests to the actor the need to do physically or to react to something. Consider what sort of actions the actor playing Juliet must make here in order for the words to make sense:

Juliet: What's here? A cup, closed in my true love's hand?
Poison, I see, hath been his timeless end.
O churl! Drunk all, and left no friendly drop
To help me after? I will kiss thy lips.
Haply some poison yet doth hang on them
To make me die with a restorative.
Thy lips are warm!

Effective oral communication involves suiting the action to the word and the word to the action. Sometimes, though, communication occurs purely through the use of non-verbal signs that are integrated with speech. Consider what is happening here between a drama teacher and her class:

Can you just come and sit round here and then Will's gonna . . . (*two second pause*) Will's got the character of Jack and I've just I've asked some other people as well and they're gonna perform their bits. It's just so that in this devising process you can look at other people's work and then we can say 'right, well, that was really effective', so it might help you do what you want to do or you can say 'well, actually, well that could have been a little bit improved', so it's gonna help you in your devising . . . (*four second pause*) . . . OK? . . . It's gonna help you in your devising process as well so it is work in process: it's not like we're expecting a finished piece.

Seasoned classroom observers will doubtless recognise the purpose of the pauses here and the sort of visual signifiers that probably accompanied them. In fact, the first short pause is used to give the class a moment to arrange themselves. The teacher, while standing still, sweeps the class with her eyes and checks that she has gained attention before continuing. The second longer pause followed by a very quiet 'OK' involves the teacher standing absolutely still and looking placidly at one boy who is still shuffling. The visual signifier serves its purpose and the boy settles. The stillness and the look is, in effect, a deictical sign (it draws attention to something), a discourse marker (it signals that she has not finished) and a modal expression (it reinforces the teacher–pupil relationship). In order to serve all these functions the physical signing needed to be precise. Understanding and encouraging the precise use of signs is the bedrock of a great deal of drama practice. The argument here is that exploring these aspects of oral communication benefits all pupils in their understanding of and ability to utilise speech and listen effectively.

Active investigation

A very simple way of helping pupils to understand the nature and function of deictical speech is to compare the difference between when it is used and when it isn't.

Working in groups of three, one pupil (A) is given the task of instructing another (B) to move an object from one part of the room to another. The third pupil (C) acts as a scorer and referee. In the first part of the exercise A decides what is to be moved, to where and how. B is not allowed to ask any questions and may only move exactly as he or she is told. Pupil C tries to keep a tally of how many times A says 'there, here, this, that' etc. and also notes instances of A pointing, gesticulating and demonstrating.

In the second part of the exercise A must only give precise verbal instructions. If C hears any deictical words he or she intervenes by making a game-show klaxon sound. A must then try to find a more precise way of verbalising what he or she wants B to do.

Purposefully vague language

Carter (2002: 6) uses the term 'purposefully vague language' to describe words or phrases that 'soften' spoken English. Words and phrases such as 'stuff', 'thing', 'you know' and 'sort of' serve a number of important functions in speech. Like modal expressions, vague language can help to establish a relationship between speaker and listener where the speaker is trying to avoid seeming too authoritative or assertive. Like ellipsis and deixis, vague language assumes a shared understanding, and like spoken clauses it can be used to emphasise a point. In such instances the vagueness is deliberate. Consider the different functions the use of vague language serves in this extract from Conor McPherson's play *The Weir*:

> Finbar: She was after, **come on now**, she was after being down in a friend of hers' house or this. And they were after doing the . . . Ouija board. And she phoned her mother to come and collect her. They said they were getting after a spirit or this, **you know**, and she was scared, saying it was after her.
>
> And I obviously thought, this was a load of bollocks, **you know**? If you'll . . . excuse the language Valerie. But here was the mother saying she'd gone and picked her up. I mean, **like**, **sorry**, but I thought it was all a bit mad. But on the way back they'd seen something, like the mother had seen it as well. Like a dog on the road, running with the car and running after it. Like there's dogs all around here, Valerie, **you know**? The farmers have them. There was a big dog up there, Jack, that Willie McDermott had that time.
>
> Jack: **Oh Jaysus, yeah**, it was like a, if you saw it from a distance, you'd think it was a little horse. It was huge.
>
> Jim: Saxon.
>
> Finbar: That was it. Saxon.
>
> Jim: It was an Irish Wolfhound. He got it off a fella in the north.
>
> Finbar: Yeah, it was huge. You'd be used to seeing dogs all around the place. All kinds, but they'd be tame, **like**.

'Purposefully vague language' can also act in much the same way as stabilisers such as 'er' or 'um'. In live situations its use buys the speaker time to think about what they are saying and the effect they are having on their audience.

What happens when attention is drawn to the use of vague language is that, as with the other features of spoken language, it becomes immediately apparent how the overuse of such utterances quickly becomes annoying and detracts from the content of what is being said. In other words, there is a need to recognise that the features of oral language outlined here can be marshalled to tremendous effect in communicating sense to a given audience. Conversely, not recognising how these features work and failing to use them judiciously can result in speech becoming incomprehensible.

There is a link between vague language in the verbal sense and vague physical language. Just as some gestures are highly refined and purposeful – for example, the use of a pause and look or pointing with a finger to an object – others simply denote, sometimes unintentionally, more general attitudes or states of tension. In the context of a rehearsed dramatic performance, the use of gesture is carefully considered in order to make it serve a deliberate communicative function; vagueness is replaced with intentionality in order to add to the meaning rather than detract or confuse.

What is being suggested here is that attempting to apply the grammatical conventions of writing to oral speech is unlikely to result in effective oral communication. Instead, what is needed is the development of an ability to select and use different features of spoken language, along with visual and aural signifiers chosen to suit a given audience. In this, perhaps more than in any other way, the use of practical drama and the study of dramatic literature can improve pupils' use and understanding of spoken English by drawing attention to its features and effects and creating situations in which they can interrogate and practise what constitutes appropriate speech in different contexts.

CHAPTER

6

Words and actions

Visual and aural literacy

THE PRINCIPLE ARGUMENT of Chapter 5 is that attending only to the choice of words does not constitute a secure grounding for effective oral communication. In live situations the audience of any utterance is receiving a plethora of other signals that may help or hinder the interpretation of what is being said. Although written in relation specifically to drama, J. L. Styan's words hold true for all speakers and audiences: 'Dramatic meaning cannot lie in words alone, but in voices and the tone of voices, in the pace of speaking and the silences between the gesture and expression of the actor, physical distinctions between him and others' (Styan 1975: 26). Any attempt to codify exactly how these signifiers work into a comprehensive grammar of oral communication is doomed to failure. As John O'Toole (1992: 199) has noted: 'The trouble which semiotics has found . . . is that language in drama is so polyfunctional that analysis quickly becomes incomprehensibly obscure to anyone but the analyst, or turns into counting sand – endless and useless.' Nevertheless, in the teaching of speaking and listening it is useful to help young people to understand the range and nature of the signifiers that accompany the spoken word. Discussing these factors and reflecting on them in practical exercises heightens children's awareness of their importance. The classification in Table 6.1, adapted from the work of Kowzan (1968: 73), can usefully serve as a framework for analysing any type of spoken communication, be it an everyday occurrence, improvised or rehearsed.

This classification demonstrates that, alongside the spoken text – that is, what is being said and in what way – an audience will be aware of other contextual factors. Some of these factors may be controlled by the speaker. In an interview situation, for example, the candidate may well have thought very carefully about how to dress and what make-up to wear. Giving a presentation at a sales conference might involve the careful use of lighting and props, such as examples of the

TABLE 6.1 A classification for analysing spoken communication

1 Choice of words 2 Intonation	Spoken text	Auditive signs	Temporal
3 Facial expressions 4 Gestures 5 Movement 6 Position in space	Physical text	Visual signs	Temporal and spatial
7 Physical appearance 8 Costume	Physical text	Visual signs	Spatial
9 Setting 10 Lighting 11 Use of objects	Visual text	Visual signs	Temporal and spatial
12 Sound	Aural text	Auditive signs	Temporal

Source: adapted from Kowzan (1968: 73)

product, as well as music chosen to set a particular mood. A skilled communicator will be able to make deliberate use of facial expressions and gestures to emphasise points and recognise the power of stillness, and will move deliberately as opposed to shuffling from one foot to another. Positioning is also of vital importance; we all know how uncomfortable it can be for someone to get too close to us when they are speaking and how difficult it is to listen to someone when they are speaking with their back to us or are standing by a window when the sun is shining through it and silhouetting them.

Notwithstanding the way speakers may predetermine what they want to say and how, they sometimes have to contend with factors beyond their control: the room is too small, too big, too hot, too cold, too bright, too dim. The furniture is uncomfortable. Not enough time has been allowed to say all that has been prepared. A gang of workmen is digging up the road outside. Beyond this, of course, one can never be completely sure that the sense of the presentation will come across in the way intended. What if the audience interprets personal presentation as being arrogant rather than confident, weak rather than modest, garish rather than colourful? The best a speaker can do is to try to identify what the needs of the audience are likely to be in any given context and then select a verbal, visual and aural grammar to suit. In discussing the nature of 'politeness', Bourdieu (1991: 19) argues that it is not an exceptional phenomenon: 'Tact is nothing other than the capacity of the speaker to assess market conditions accurately and to produce linguistic expressions which are appropriate to them, that is, which are suitably euphemised.' Effective speech involves the fine-tuning of visual signifiers. Conversely, effective listening involves watching carefully. Bourdieu's political critique of language reminds us, though, that such tuning is contingent upon class-based assumptions of what is deemed acceptable in any given situation.

Active investigation

Deconstructing recordings of films and television shows in terms of the different factors affecting the way speech is interpreted makes those facets of oral communication that we normally accept subtextually explicit.

- Show the pupils an extract from the comedy series *The Office*. A particularly useful example is when egocentric office manager David Brent presents a training course.

- Discuss the assumptions that David Brent has made about his audience and the decisions he has taken in preparing his presentation.

- Ask the pupils to devise a scene in which someone misreads a situation by making inappropriate choices in how they present themselves.

- Use forum theatre techniques to explore what might constitute more effective presentational strategies.

The voice as instrument

> The voice is the means by which, in everyday life, you communicate with other people, and though, of course, how you present yourself – your posture, movement, dress and involuntary gesture – gives an impression of your personality, it is through the speaking voice that you convey your precise thoughts and feelings. This also involves the amount of vocabulary you have at your disposal and the particular words you choose. It follows, therefore, that the more responsive and efficient the voice is, the more accurate it will be to your intentions.

(Berry 1973: 7)

What Cecily Berry, a leading voice coach, is referring to here is diction in both senses of the word. That is: 'manner of enunciating in speaking or singing; choice of words and phrases in speech or writing' (*Oxford English Dictionary*).

Helping pupils to acquire an extended vocabulary and ensuring that they are able to say what they want to say clearly is a responsibility for all teachers, and an understanding of what terms such as 'diction' imply will help them in this work. Neither accent nor dialect necessarily militates against speaking clearly and expressively. Simply telling children to 'speak properly' is largely meaningless unless 'properly' is defined. In practice, notions of 'proper spoken English' are all too often associated with RP, an accent that is used by relatively few people but is sometimes held to have a disproportionate status. RP can, in some contexts, seem as inappropriate and grating as any other pronunciation, with the result that what is being said gets lost because of the way it is said. 'Speaking properly' may be better defined as speaking in a manner that suits the context in such a way as to endeavour to convey the sense of what is being said as accurately as possible. In this light it is useful to consider the voice in much the same way as a musical instrument, which can be regulated in terms of volume, pitch, tone and resonance. It is the difference between picking the strings of a guitar and manically strumming it. Considering each vowel and consonant as a separate note produces speech that is more tuneful and easier to listen to than a cacophony where notes sit on each other or are missed out altogether. This does not imply that all children should have formal speech training, but it does argue for a regime of correction when not to correct would leave the child unable to communicate effectively. Imagine, for example, a child who habitually dismissed the letter t from his written work. Would his submission that ''he ca' sa' on 'he ma'' be acceptable?

Learning to play an instrument requires practising with the instrument. Similarly, translating a sound that you can hear in your head into something others can hear and make sense of involves being able to manipulate physical processes in subtle ways. Just as young musicians practise scales and changes in order to extend their repertoire, young speakers will benefit from physically playing with their voices. What becomes apparent when students are given the opportunity to use their voices in a variety of ways is that new and often unexpected meanings emerge: 'you know what you want to communicate, but in the physical act of making sound, meanings take on a new dimension' (Berry 1973: 13). This phenomenon is never more apparent than when working in the field of drama, where the most subtle changes of tone or pitch can be held up for inspection and interrogated for inference. Beyond this it should be recognised that simply speaking new words out loud can contribute to a child's understanding of their semantic meaning. There's little reason to suspect that many pupils will turn up to a lesson on *Hamlet* knowing what phrases such as 'cursed hebona' and 'leperous distilment' mean or what happened to Old Hamlet when 'a most instant tetter barked about'. However, by getting pupils to play with the sounds of the words and attend to what saying them out loud does to them physically, then the semantic meaning can become clear without the aid of footnotes.

Active investigation

A simple and effective way of helping pupils to understand how they can manipulate their voices is to offer them a number of binary oppositions to work with.

- Introduce the class to the idea of personification and discuss examples such as Walt Disney's *Beauty and the Beast* and *Toy Story*.

- Ask them to consider how they might personify items of furniture in an old house. By way of modelling the technique ask them to suggest how a grandfather clock might be portrayed. Is it light or heavy, young or old, bright or dull? How does selecting from these opposites affect the way the character stands, moves and speaks?

- Give the pupils a chance to develop a depiction of another inanimate object by selecting from oppositions. For example, how would they depict a doormat? Would it be smooth or spiky, content or complaining, fast or slow? Working first on a physical representation, the pupils should move on to giving an appropriate voice to their character.

Appropriateness to context

Notions of what is or is not appropriate to any given situation are contingent on the value system at work within that situation. It is all too easy simply to accept these systems without questioning where they have come from. There are pitfalls, though, to imagining that everyone else shares the same set of values. Teaching children to realise the effect their speech has on others, and appreciating why they are affected in different ways when they listen to others, requires focusing on personal perceptions of appropriateness and how these link to perceptions of social norms.

By its very nature, drama is an invaluable medium for exploring different social occasions. As an art form it necessarily involves people communicating with one another in the process of making and performing. What is being communicated in a great deal of drama work is precisely how people respond in different social conditions. Contextualising talk in this manner has been found to be a more effective way of helping students to develop their language skills than setting decontextualised exercises designed specifically to improve or assess the use of the spoken word (Dixon 1988: 42). Questions to be explored in order to understand the relationship between appropriateness and context include:

- What purpose does the speaker wish to fulfil?

- How do they perceive the values and needs of their audience?

- To what extent is the physical setting conducive to purposes and needs being fulfilled?

Once again, what needs to be addressed is not just how the speaker goes about meeting his or her intentions through an act of physical communication, but how that act is perceived by an audience in the environmental context.

Active investigation

Ask the pupils to suggest different ways of completing the following sentences and discuss the results:

> . . . is a good place to . . .
> . . . is a bad place to . . .

For example:

> 'A secluded moonlit balcony is a good place to declare your love for someone.'
> 'The school assembly hall is a bad place to reveal a personal secret.'

The exercise can highlight which values are shared and why and so frames the concept of 'appropriateness' by way of identifying how an unspoken social contract may be transgressed.

When the sentences have been completed ask pupils to improvise short conversations that take place in suitable and unsuitable arenas.

Register

Used in the context of speaking, the term 'register' encompasses the choice of both specific vocabulary and syntax. It can also incorporate the choice of specific non-verbal signifiers such as movement and gesture. The concept of register is closely associated with appropriateness and needs to be introduced in order to further children's understanding of it.

Both vocabulary and syntax act as strong signifiers of character and situation. Teachers, for example, might be easily recognised by their use of words and terms that fall outside the range of most people not involved in education: Ofsted, Key Stage 3, SATs, house assembly, detention, homework, markbook, TES, form group, curriculum. Within the more general culture of education, sub-groups will have their own highly particularised registers, understood by those 'in the know' and thoroughly perplexing to outsiders. Think, for example, of the way different rooms, groups or occasions in your school are referred to. In essence, this highly localised register is akin to a dialect and can reflect social class as well as regionality. Consider, for example, the difference between the terms 'homework' and 'prep', or 'non-uniform day' and 'mufti day', a term originating from the military in the days of empire.

Alongside this specific vocabulary, there are a great many phrases that people would instantly recognise as 'teacher talk': 'Johnny, don't do that!' 'Get your books out.' 'This is your time that you're wasting.'

Active investigation

Ask pupils to collect words and phrases associated with different professionals. What sort of things, for example, do car mechanics, doctors, hairdressers or dentists say?

Having gathered together examples, ask pupils to work in pairs and give them the task of indicating to each other who and where they are as quickly as possible through what they say. For example, one pupil takes a seat and initiates a conversation by saying, 'Well, I think I'll just have the usual trim please and perhaps put the highlights back in.' The partner must then signal that she has understood the register by offering a suitable reply: 'Do want your nails done today as well?' Having established the situation, the pupils swap over and start a new scene. Centring the improvisations on a chair works well, as it helps the pupils to find different situations quickly. The chair may be in a dentist's, on an aircraft, in a palace or perhaps in an execution chamber!

Encourage pupils to experiment with the way language jars when there is a mismatch between register and context. What would happen, for example, if one professional spoke in a register belonging to another professional? Here is a transcript of one pair of Year 9 pupils' work where the conceit was that hairdressers spoke as if they were lawyers:

A. For my next customer I would like to call Mr Frederick Brown to the chair. Now Mr Brown, place your right hand on the scissors and repeat after me 'I Frederick Brown do solemnly swear . . .

B. I Frederick Brown do solemnly swear . . .

A: . . . to sit still throughout these proceedings.'

B: . . . to sit still throughout these proceedings.

A: Now, Mr Brown, perhaps you could tell us why you are here this morning.

B: Well, I had a look in the mirror and said to myself, Fred, it's time you had your hair cut.

A: And is that all you saw in the mirror this morning, Mr Brown?

B: Well, I thought I could do with a shave as well to be honest.

A: Take a close look at this comb, Mr Brown, and tell me what you see between its teeth.

B: Um . . . some little white bits.

A: Some little white bits? Come, come Mr Brown. Tell us what those little white bits are.

B: (quietly) Dandruff.

A: Speak up Mr Brown.

B: Dandruff.

A: Yes, Mr Brown. Dandruff. I put it to you that when you looked in the mirror this morning you saw that you needed more than a haircut didn't you? You knew that you needed a wash with medicated shampoo. Isn't that so, Mr Brown?

B: Well I . . .

A: I think I can rest my case. You will be taken from this chair and sent to the sink where your hair will be washed until it is clean. Call the next customer.

7

Using playscripts as models of speech

Speaking for a purpose

THE KEY STAGE 3 *Literacy across the Curriculum* folder (DfEE 2001b) provides a list of types of non-fiction writing and interestingly encourages teachers to provide pupils with an oral example of each type:

- Instructions: recipes, giving directions.

- Recount: science experiment write-up, match commentary.

- Explanation: the rain cycle, how erosion occurs.

- Information: food in Britain, the properties of mercury.

- Persuasion: advertisement, manifesto.

- Discursive writing: 'discuss' essays, magazine article.

- Analysis: literary criticism, analytical essay.

A similar list can be drawn up to identify types of speech. However, in the teaching of speaking and listening, like writing, the project is not simply to identify which mode of speech is being used and why, but to consider its appropriateness to a situation and the effect it has on its recipients. Interrogating the interaction between speaker and listener effectively draws attention to *how* the speaker is communicating: what words are being used in what order, and what else the speaker is doing while speaking to provoke a response. One way of analysing this dynamic is to consider how playwrights capture contextualised interactions.

In this chapter a number of short extracts from plays are presented to reflect different modes of speech in action. Dramatic dialogue appropriates modes of everyday speech. Unlike real life speech, it has been written first in order to be spoken. Words and phrases are carefully chosen by the playwright in order to add to the overall meaning of the play and the construction of unique characters. In this sense, dramatic dialogue is a highly falsified version of natural speech. Nevertheless, a study of the way playwrights capture the essence of spoken communication is a valuable resource for the teaching of speaking and listening precisely because the modes of speech selected by the playwright to serve a given purpose are often clearly defined and more easily recognisable than in transcripts of recorded live speech. Furthermore, the fact that plays are written and published means that English and drama teachers have ready access to a wide range of exemplar material. Using extracts from plays in this way not only broadens pupils' knowledge of dramatic literature but allows them opportunities to investigate the additional meanings that arise when speech is accompanied by action rather than studied on the page alone.

Instructing: *Lives Worth Living* by Lawrence Evans and Jane Nash

Lives Worth Living was devised as a piece of theatre in education with the intention of raising awareness about attitudes to the disabled and people with learning difficulties. Mark and Julie are on holiday shortly after their mother's death. Much as Julie loves and protects Mark, she knows that she cannot always be there for him and that he must learn to look after himself as well as possible, something the institutions he has been in have failed to help him with. Julie's explanation of how to tie a pair of shoelaces seems packed with ellipsis, stabilisers and vague language, yet given the visual and physical context and the use of deixis, it all becomes perfectly clear.

Julie: (*Notices his untied laces*) Oh look at state of ya! You'll trip up. Sit down.
Mark: What?
Julie: Sit down. (*They sit.*)

(*Insistently.*) Now watch!

Takes one set of laces and demonstrates tying them. MARK *watches intently.*

Now you got your two laces right – cross 'em over – now that one has got to go in there like that, right? – now take both ends and pull – like that see – now you're going to make a loop with this one right – so watch, watch – there's your finger right – now make a loop round your finger and hold it at the bottom, right – now this one has got to go all the way round the outside – so, watch, watch – right. Now this is the hard bit – you've got to make another loop by pushing that through there with your finger – right, so you got a loop there and a loop there – now pull gently – there, see – now you have a go.
Mark: What?
Julie: You heard!

There follows a long moment between them. JULIE *is almost daring him to have a go.* MARK *glances between* JULIE *and his unlaced shoe. He decides to have a go.*

Throughout it is extraordinarily difficult for him: instruction – assimilation – carrying out instruction.

> Two laces – cross 'em over – cross 'em – right – now that one goes in there – go on – right – now take hold of the ends – the other one too – right – now pull – now you've got to make a loop like I showed you – round your finger – right – well hold it at the bottom – right – now that one goes all the way round – gently – make sure that loop stays up – there – now you've got to push that one through there like that – come on, you do it! – right now you've got the two loops, one there and one there – now pull – pull – THERE!

Mark: (*triumphant*) YEAH!!

- Read Julie's first speech out to the class starting with 'cross 'em over': in other words, take out the reference to the laces. Ask the class if they understand what is going on from the words alone.

- Ask the class to work in pairs with one of the pupils teaching the other how to tie a pair of laces as if it is a new experience for the second pupil. Show them this extract and talk about both how well it captures the difficulty of instructing and how accurate a representation of this sort of situation it is.

- Look at the number of times Julie says 'right' and talk about what different functions this one word seems to have in the context of her teaching Mark how to tie his laces.

- Prepare a simple drawing, such as a house with a tree at the side. Divide the class into pairs and have the pupils sit back to back. Give one pupil the drawing and the other a sheet of plain paper. Using only words, the pupil with the drawing must give the other pupil instructions for exactly what to draw. The aim should be not only to try and draw the shape but to get the proportions and the positioning on the plain sheet right as well.

Recounting: *Spoonface Steinberg* by Lee Hall

Spoonface Steinberg was originally written as a radio play but later successfully transferred to the stage, with Kathryn Hunter, an actor especially well known for her physical work, playing the eponymous role. The play consists of a monologue, interrupted by recordings of Maria Callas singing, by a seven-year-old autistic girl who is dying of cancer.

> I was never right ever since I was born – this means that I do very bad writing and that I can't speak proper and that I am backwards and that I am a special child – but why is a mystery for what they have not got an answer – but Mam said when I was born it was at a dark night and it was raining and thundery and all the cats and dogs and things were under the tables – and the wind was screeching round everywhere – and everything was

quite horrible – but I didn't mind because I was just little and I was in the hospital and Mam kissed me and when she looked at my face she noticed that it was round – and everyone came and looked at my face – and they laughed and said I was Spoonface because when they looked at my face it was round as a spoon and when you look into a spoon you see this face just like mine – and that is how I came to be Spoonface Steinberg – because my other name is Steinberg.

- Ask the class to identify words and phrases that suggest the speaker is a very young person.

- Are there some parts of the speech that could be considered to be poor in terms of standard written grammar but add poignancy to the overall effect of the speech because of this?

- How does the lack of punctuation and use of connectives add to the impact of the speech?

- Ask pupils to decide how the speech might be delivered using the binary oppositions exercise. Is Spoonface's voice big or small, fast or slow, light or dark?

- Ask pupils to imagine that the speech is being read after her death by an older person who knew Spoonface. What choices would they make about the way they used their voice to do this?

Narrating: *Sparkleshark* by Philip Ridley

Sparkleshark is a play about a boy who uses his ability to tell stories to stop a gang beating him up. In this extract members of the gang are drawn into his story and start to narrate it collectively.

Shane: . . . Let me tell you about the Witch.

Slight pause.

A million years ago I met her. On a planet far away. She was a powerful sorceress then. Her magic potion was the most potent in the universe. Savage monsters could be tamed with one whiff. I was tamed.

Slight pause.

And then, one day, she refused to answer when I called her name. I screamed so loud stars became supernova.

Slight pause.

She has spent a million years avoiding me. Fleeing each planet as I arrive. I never worked out why she loved me so much one day . . . then, the next, not at all.

Slight pause.

An egg.

Natasha: Wh . . . what?

Slight pause.

Jake: A Dragon's egg.
Polly: A Dragon's egg, yes!
Buzz: Wicked!
Speed: Awesome!
Carol: What about it?

Slight pause.

Jake: . . . the Wizard told the Prince about the Dragon. It lives in the mountain –
Polly: I've heard about this Dragon. It's got jaws like a shark.
Jake: And scales like sequins.
Polly: And this Dragon – yes, of course! – it lays eggs.
Jake: (*with Polly*) Eggs more beautiful than a million yellow flowers!
Polly: (*with Jake*) Eggs more beautiful than a million yellow flowers!

Pause.

Shane: Go to the mountains. Find the Dragon's egg. The Princess will be yours.
Buzz: But . . . won't there be two Dragons?
Speed: A Mummy and a Daddy?
Jake: It's an hermaphrodite Dragon.

Slight pause.

Half boy, half girl.

Russell: Relative of yours, Jake?

Jake: It's a ferocious Dragon. It might be covered with sequins. But each sequin is as sharp as a razor blade.

Slight pause.

Be careful, Prince.

Pause.

Russell: (*in sports commentator voice*) 'The Prince faces the challenge without fear. Is this the bravest man on earth or what? In a few incredible strides he scales the heights of the mountain.'

Climbs metal stairs.

'It's freezing cold, but is the Prince shivering? No! He's not even wearing protective clothing. Is the man mortal? We have to ask ourselves. And there . . . Is it? Yes! I believe it is! He's found it! Easy!'

Takes football from his sports bag.

The Dragon's egg!

Shane: The cold must be making the Prince hallucinate.

Pause.

Russell: 'Undeterred, the turbo-dreamboat of a Prince searches again! What stamina! What grit! And now – Yes!'

Lifts an old lampshade in air.

The Dragon's egg!

- Help the class to pick out examples of ellipsis here that, taken out of context, would mean little, but that make perfect sense given the preceding line or action.

- Sometimes the story is told in the first person ('A million years ago I met her'), and sometimes in the third person ('The Wizard told the Prince about the Dragon'). Similarly, the tense changes from past tense ('one day she refused to answer') to present ('It's freezing cold, but is the Prince shivering?') and on occasion to future ('Go to the mountains. Find the Dragon's egg. The Princess will be yours'). Usually, fairy stories are just told in the past tense. Discuss what slipping from one tense to another in this instance adds to the sense of drama.

- Ask the pupils to work in small groups to retell a well known fairy story. Each pupil must change the tense from the one before. For example: 'One day Little Red Riding Hood set off on a trip through the forest. She was going to see her Grandma' (past tense). 'She is walking through the woods. She sees a wolf. Now the wolf jumps out in front of her. He speaks. She is going with him off the path' (present). 'She will be tempted to pick some flowers. She will get lost. The wolf will get to Grandma's cottage before her' (future).

- Change the exercise to focus on the person, e.g. 'I am walking through the woods. I see a wolf. He is coming closer to me' (first person present). 'You will be tempted away from the path. You will get lost and the wolf will beat you to your Grandma's cottage' (second person future). 'She arrived at Grandma's cottage and went in. She found Grandma in bed but something was strange about her' (third person past – the usual storytelling mode).

- Working with the whole group in a circle, try telling a story in different modes, e.g. 'Red Riding Hood set off to take her Grandma some lunch one day. She said goodbye to her mother and skipped merrily off towards the forest' (narration). 'The forest was a dazzling green. The sunlight filtered down through the leaves making beautiful patterns across the path. But as she went in further it became darker and darker and it became a little more difficult for Red Riding Hood to see exactly where she was going' (description). 'This was because the forest was very big. It had been there for thousands of years. Red Riding Hood needed to go through the darkest part because that was the quickest way to Grandma's house' (explanation). But she senses danger. She hears the soft padding of a large animal. The animal leaps out in front of her. She jumps with fright. The animal speaks' (action). 'This is because the tale of Red Riding Hood is a fairy tale and animals can speak in fairy tales. Fairy tales aren't real and are full of magic so all sorts of things can happen in them' (explanation).

■ Ask the pupils to work in groups and use a range of first, second and third person forms and different tenses to make an enactment of a fairy story more engaging. In reflecting on the work, draw attention to the way pace and tone tend to change depending on which person and tense is being used

Explaining: *The Life of Galileo* by Bertolt Brecht

A major part of Brecht's project as a dramatist was to make the audience actively think about what they were seeing and hearing. Theatre, for him, had a clear educational purpose. While *The Life of Galileo* appears at first glance simply to trace the events that led to the scientist's falling out of favour with the Church and his subsequent recanting of his findings, the play also works as a critical analysis of the relationship between science and the state. It encourages audiences to think about moral responsibility and the dangers of either taking things at face value or accepting things as truth simply because authority tells you they are the truth. In this scene, Galileo helps his young assistant to realise that what appears obvious may have another explanation.

Galileo: Do you understand what I told you yesterday?

Andrea: What? All that about Kippernicus and his rotation?

Galileo: Yes.

Andrea: No. How do you expect me to understand it? It's very difficult, and I'm only eleven next October.

Galileo: I particularly want *you* to understand it too. That's why I'm working and buying expensive books instead of paying the milkman – so that people can understand it.

Andrea: But I can *see* that the sun is in a different place in the evening from what it was in the morning. So it can't be standing still. Never, never.

Galileo: You *see*! What do you see? You see nothing. You can only goggle. Goggling is not seeing

He sets the iron wash-basin in the middle of the room.

Well, that's the sun. Sit down.

Andrea sits on the one chair. Galileo stands behind him.

> Where is the sun, right or left?

Andrea: Left.

Galileo: And how can it get to your right?

Andrea: If you carry it to the right, of course.

Galileo: Is that the only way?

He picks him up with the chair and rotates him through a semicircle.

> Now where is the sun?

Andrea: On the right.

Galileo: And did it move?

Andrea: No! *It* didn't.

Galileo: Well, what did move?

Andrea: I did.

Galileo: (*shouts*) Wrong, you idiot! The chair.

Andrea: But I went with it!

Galileo: Of course you did. The chair is the earth. You are sitting on it.

- In this extract, Galileo manages to reveal a truth to Andrea by matching words and actions. Read the extract through with the pupils and discuss how much sense Galileo's explanation would make if there were no actions to go with it.

- In pairs, ask the pupils to take it in turns to try to explain how to get from one part of the school to another. The role of the listener is to note how the speaker uses different strategies, such as pointing and gesturing, or questioning the listener to check that he or she can visualise key points on the route.

- Working in groups of four, get the pupils to improvise a scene in which one character asks another for directions and duly receives them. The game is that the speakers do not use their own arms to gesture. Instead, they stand with their arms behind their backs. Their classmates stand behind them and extend their arms forward in order to make the appropriate signs. This is an age old party gag but usefully draws attention to the role that gesturing and pointing plays when explaining.

Persuading: *Oh What a Lovely War* by Theatre Workshop

Oh What a Lovely War was devised by Joan Littlewood's company to show the absurdity of the First World War by creating a montage of scenes based on real events. The scenes often seem comical but the comedy is juxtaposed with a slide show and electronic news board displaying disturbing images and statistics. The use of popular songs from the time adds to the tragic irony.

In this scene, the suffragette and pacifist activist Sylvia Pankhurst tries to make a persuasive speech against the war but it is perhaps her use of language that stops her achieving her aim.

Mrs Pankhurst: Now, before talking to you all, I should like to read you a letter from my friend George Bernard Shaw.

Second man: Who's he when he's at home?

First woman: Ain't it disgusting?

Mrs Pankhurst: He says: 'The men of this country are being sacrificed to the blunders of boobies, the cupidity of capitalists, the ambition of conquerors, the lusts and lies and rancours of bloodthirsts that love war, because it opens their prison doors and sets them on the throne of power and popularity.'

Third man: Now give us a song!

Mrs Pankhurst: For the second time peace is being offered to the sorely tried people of the civilized world . . .

Second man: Hallo.

Mrs Pankhurst: . . . at the close of 1915 President Wilson proposed an immediate armistice; to be followed by a peace conference . . .

Second man: Hallo!

Mrs Pankhurst: . . . in April of this year, Germany herself proposed peace . . .

Second man: Hallo! Hallo!

Mrs Pankhurst: . . . the peace movements are strong in England, France and the United States; and in Germany. In the Reichstag . . .

Second man: Who's he when he's at home?

Mrs Pankhurst: . . . the peace groups are active and outspoken; the exact terms of Germany's offer have never been made known to us and I should like to ask Lloyd George what his war aims are.

First woman: I should like to ask you what your old man has for dinner!

Mrs Pankhurst: . . . the politicians chatter like imbeciles while civilization bleeds to death.

Third man: You're talking like a traitor. Pacifists are traitors.

Mrs Pankhurst: I ask that gentleman . . .

Third man: Don't ask me . . . 'Cos I don't know nothing . . . I'm stupid.

Mrs Pankhurst: . . . to consider the plight of the civilized world after another year: you do not know what you do and the statesmen wash their hands of the whole affair . . .

Fourth man: Why don't you wash your face!

Second man: Douglas Haig's got them on the run.

Mrs Pankhurst: Who tells you this? *The Times* . . .

Second man: He's got them going.

Mrs Pankhurst: . . . the newspaper that refuses to publish the pacifist letters, and distorts the facts of our so-called victories. We are killing off slowly but surely the best of the male population . . .

First woman: Here! Don't you address them words to me . . .
Second woman: Here! Don't you address them words to her . . .

- Consider what indicators there are here that while Mrs Pankhurst and her audience are both speaking English, they are not speaking the same kind of English.

- Ask pupils to pick out any words or phrases in Mrs Pankhurst's speech that may help to explain why she seems unable to get the listeners on her side.

- It is one thing to prepare a speech by actually writing it down or carefully thinking it through in advance. However, unless speakers can adjust what they say and the way they say it to the needs of the audience they are unlikely to get their message across. A useful exercise is to ask pupils to prepare a persuasive speech for other members of the class. The task for the audience is to let the speaker get going but then to start interjecting with questions and comments. The speaker must decide whether to ignore or reply to these. The focus of reflective discussion after this exercise is to consider what happens to the audience's attitude when their comments and questions are always ignored, and what happens to the content and structure of the speech when they are always replied to.

- Effective oral communication is often largely dependent on the speaker's ability to make eye contact and give every member of the audience the impression that they are being spoken to personally. An exercise designed to help pupils develop this ability involves them working in groups of six to eight. The pupils take it in turns to start making a speech about something they feel strongly about. As they speak they must try to make regular eye contact with every member of the group. Each member of the audience group silently counts from one to ten slowly. If they reach ten before the speaker has looked at them they stand up. Every time the speaker looks at them they must start their count again. The aim for the speaker is, of course, to say what they want to say without having anyone standing up.

Discussing: *A Number* by Caryl Churchill

A Number explores the issue of human cloning. Salter, a man in his early sixties, is confronted by his son Bernard (B2), who has discovered that he is a clone of his elder brother, whom Salter gave up for adoption. Furthermore, Bernard has discovered that he is not the only clone. As the play moves on, Salter encounters both his eldest son (B1) whose cells were originally cloned and another clone. Salter's past and his attitudes towards his different offspring are revealed entirely through conversational dialogue.

B2:   I think I'd like to meet one. It's an adventure isn't it and you're part of science. I wouldn't be frightened to meet any number.

Salter: I don't know.

B2:   They're all your sons.

Salter: I don't want any number of sons, thank you, you're plenty, I'm fine.

B2:   Maybe after they've found everything out they'll let us meet. They'll have a party for us, we can

Salter: I'm not going to drink with those doctors. But maybe you're right, you're right, take it in a positive spirit.

B2:   There is a thing

Salter: what's that?

B2:   a thing that puzzles me a little

Salter: what's that?

B2:   I did get the impression and I know I may be wrong because maybe I was in shock but I got the impression there was this batch and we were all in it. I was in it.

Salter: No because you're my son.

B2:   No but we were all

Salter: I explained already

B2:   but I wasn't being quite so open with you because I'm confused because it's a shock but I want to know what happened

Salter: they stole.

B2:   no but what happened

Salter: I don't

B2:   because they said that none of us was the original.

Salter: They said that?

B2:   I think

Salter: I think you're mistaken because you're confused

B2:   you think

Salter: you need to get back to them

B2:   well I'll do that. But I think that's what they meant

Salter: it's not what they meant

B2:   OK. But that's my impression, that none of us is original.

■ Keeping a conversation going clearly requires listening to what is being said and responding. Turn taking is essential, but what often occurs is that each speaker has their own agenda of things that they want to say. This means that rather than following a single progressive line, conversations tend to jump about as speakers acknowledge what they have heard but then pursue their own line of thought. Read this extract through with the pupils and identify those moments when one or other speaker seems to refer back to an earlier point rather than just responding to the preceding line.

■ Choose an issue such as human cloning as the subject of a debate. Ask each pupil in the class to adopt a simple position for or against the principle of cloning. In the first instance each pupil should state either 'yes' or 'no'. The role of the teacher is then to conduct the debate by asking first for a point in favour of cloning, then a point against, and so on. It is imperative that a point for is always followed by a point against and that the structure and turn taking is adhered to. Make the exercise more complex by insisting that each new speaker must acknowledge the point that has just been made somehow before making their own point. If they fail to do this they lose their turn and someone else is invited to have their say. Following this exercise, discuss what skills were needed in order to follow and join in the debate. For example, to what extent did pupils find it difficult to listen to new arguments when they were burning to make a point of their own? How did each new speaker acknowledge the previous point and how did they then link back to what they wanted to say?

■ Discuss how Caryl Churchill uses punctuation to try to capture the flavour of a real conversation.

Analysing and questioning: *The Biko Inquest* by Jon Blair and Norman Fenton

Although *The Biko Inquest* was staged as a play, all the dialogue was taken from the court transcript of the inquest into the death in police custody of South African political leader Steve Biko in 1977. Courts of law are, in many ways, like theatres. Costume and proxemics play a large part in the way characters and relationships are defined. In terms of modes of speech, court transcripts provide an interesting case study. Much of what is said can be classified as 'written speech', in that both barristers and defendants will have carefully prepared what they want to say in advance. What the skilful attorney tries to do, however, is either to throw witnesses off their 'prepared' text in order to reveal something they would rather not say, or keep them on text in order to stop them saying something that would damage the case. In a chat show interview the questions are usually designed to provide guests with a chance to say what they want. Lawyers' questions, like those of political journalists, are crafted in order to analyse the testimony and position the witness or interviewee. Unlike a social conversation, which might meander from one subject to another, talk in the courtroom is like a game of verbal chess.

Kentridge: You say that after he threw the chair at you he flew at Warrant-officer Beneke with his fist flying?
Snyman: Yes, he was absolutely beside himself.
Kentridge: Yes, someone used the word 'berserk'?
Snyman: Yes.

Kentridge: He was like a madman?

Snyman: Correct.

Kentridge: And you say it took five of you to bring him under control?

Snyman: Correct.

Kentridge: By the way, Major Snyman, could you give us your height and weight?

Snyman: I'm 6 foot 3 inches and 200 pounds.

Kentridge: And your colleagues, Major Snyman, would you agree that they are all well-built men?

Snyman: I would.

Kentridge: And you only subdued him with difficulty?

Snyman: Yes. In the struggle we all fell over the table and fell to the ground wrestling.

Kentridge: Even after you got him to the ground, it took a couple of minutes to get the handcuffs and leg irons onto him?

Snyman: Yes, he was like a wild animal, acting crazy.

Kentridge: And even when the handcuffs and leg irons were on him he went on struggling against them, is that right?

Snyman: Correct, he was in a fury.

Kentridge: In the course of that struggle, did anyone hit him, hit Biko?

Snyman: No.

Kentridge: No. We have already learned that you Security Police don't keep incident books and yet I believe you went to the trouble to visit the local police station to note in their book a description of this struggle. Could you read us that entry.

Snyman: '. . . the detainee was aggressive; he lashed out and went berserk and threw one of the chairs at Major Snyman: then he attacked other members of the team with his fist and was eventually overcome by the team. During a severe struggle he fell with his head against a wall . . .'

Kentridge: Just a minute, Major, in this case you have made three affidavits.

Snyman: Correct.

Kentridge: The four members of your squad who were present at this wrestling match have each made two. Colonel Goosen has made five affidavits. All the examining doctors have between them made twelve affidavits. That adds up to twenty-eight affidavits. What I want to put to you is that in none of them including your three affidavits is there a single mention of Biko having bumped his head on the wall when he fell. Perhaps it never happened?

- Consider the different types of questions Kentridge uses. Discuss what different purposes they serve.

- Look through the extract and notice how little vague language there is. Ask the pupils to suggest why this might be.

- Similarly, consider how few examples there are of modal language but talk about the effect of the way Kentridge refers to Snyman by name and title.

8

Teaching and assessing speaking and listening

Organising the classroom

Effective speaking and listening work is not only dependent on the careful selection of materials and preparation of activities, but also requires a consideration of what physical conditions will best suit the intended activities. Chapter 6 argues that how what is said is actually perceived can have as much to do with lighting and setting as with the choice of words and how they are delivered. As Bullock (DES 1975: 526) pointed out, creating a stimulating classroom environment will not, of itself, develop the child's ability to use language. On the contrary, if the focus of the lesson is to be on what is being said and how, then the teacher will need to ensure that, as far as possible, the room and its inhabitants are organised in such a way as to minimise distractions.

On entering the secondary school most children are likely to have a good deal of experience of oral work. Some of this will have involved formal presentation in assemblies and plays, for example. Activities such as 'circle time' will have given them a grounding in discussion and sharing ideas through talk, while group tasks across the curriculum will have provided opportunities for persuading, negotiating and explaining in their peer groups. However, English and drama teachers in the secondary school cannot assume that new pupils are cognisant with the conventions they have been using, what skills they have started to employ or how developing knowledge of and skills in speaking and listening can enhance their learning. Speaking and listening activities should be fun but in order to improve speaking and listening skills, and consequently learn more effectively, pupils need to focus and stay on task. There is a clear danger that because such activities may not involve reading or writing they are regarded as 'easy' and so dismissed by the pupils as being enjoyable but inconsequential. In fact, given that speaking activities require children to adhere to a number of social conventions while publicly exposing a great deal about themselves, activities that fail to stimulate and challenge can have devastating effects. Poorly structured group tasks can all too easily lead to disruption and the teacher battling to regain control; such a situation transmits a number of negative messages about the value and consequence of talk. Similarly, individual tasks that fail to provide sufficient social support for the child and recognise the high stakes involved in speaking publicly can seriously undermine a child's personal confidence and, indeed, confidence in the teacher. It is not difficult to spot pupils who are unaccustomed to focused speaking and listening work and either exploit the situation or are daunted by the requirements to contribute and speak out. It is essential, therefore, that the teacher:

- ensures that the conditions in the classroom are conducive to discussion and presentation;
- establishes the rules and routines to be observed during speaking and listening work.

This will not only give the children the immediate message that the lesson has been organised and will be purposeful, but help to instil a confidence that they will be both challenged and supported.

Of course, the practicalities are that it is not always possible to have prepared the classroom in advance of the pupils' arrival. Nevertheless, if the teacher has planned how she wants the classroom organised, the pupils can be recruited to assist in this organisation. This in itself can be a valuable lesson in modelling instructive talk and teaching how to listen for key points. For example, compare the difference between 'Nancy and Rachel, move your desk back against the wall. Jacob and John, put your desk under the window' and 'You two put that there and you two move yours there'. The contrast is between written speech, where words are used with exactitude to reduce the possibility of misinterpretation, and typical oral speech, where predication is dependent on the listeners having the same subject in mind as the speaker. Both options may be effective but readers may perhaps care to think about some of their own classes and pupils and reflect for a moment on which option is most likely to bring about the desired effect of getting the desks moved quickly and without confusion.

The factors that will influence the decision for the layout of the room are:

- the size of pupil grouping;
- the amount of movement required by pupils and staff;
- use of other equipment in the room, such as video cameras, televisions and computers;
- assessment requirements;

- deployment of other staff in the room;

- provision of an area for a performance and the placing of the 'audience'.

In many lessons, there may be a need to change the layout of the room swiftly in order to move from pair work to group discussion to presentation. Valuable time and impetus will be lost if the teacher has not considered this at the planning stage. In the English classroom it is helpful to consider the presence of desks and chairs as a resource to be employed to create appropriate settings. For example, pair work focusing on questioning and interviews can be enhanced by the presence of a desk separating the pupils, while seating groups around desks or tables cabaret style can help small group discussions and investigations because listeners can only focus on the upper half of the speakers' body. The sense of formal occasion can be heightened by placing desks as in a lecture theatre or putting them all together to create a conference table. While this latter option may sound intimidating, if the reasons are made clear it can in fact add a sense of fun to presentation work because, from the pupils' point of view, the challenge 'feels' right.

In many situations it is better simply to abandon the desks by stacking them at the edge of the room and working only with chairs and a flexible open space. For activities that require significant movement, a teacher may decide to move the class to an alternative space. However, while fresh spaces offer new alternatives, the pupils may behave differently in an unfamiliar room and expectations of what constitutes appropriate behaviour will need to be reinforced even for pupils who are accustomed to the work.

The school hall and drama studio certainly offer new possibilities for speaking and listening work. Being larger and most often open spaces they offer opportunities to explore further how proxemics can affect and be utilised to enhance and change the sense of what is being said and to discover something about acoustics and projection.

Active investigation

Ask pupils new to a large space to sit with as much space as possible between them and simply listen as the teacher talks while moving around the room.

- Ask them to notice how hard it is to listen to someone who is moving around while talking. Even though the speaker may be speaking at a consistent volume the listener will experience changes in volume as they move closer or further away or turn their head to project in a different direction. (Many teachers themselves often tend to forget this and are surprised when children come up to them and ask what they have to do when, from the teacher's point of view, the explanation was perfectly clear.)

- Ask them to compare this with how much easier it is to listen to someone speaking from a commanding stationary position, such as on the stage or a rostrum block.

- Point out how, when speaking from such a position, it is necessary to talk slightly over the heads of those nearest to you in order to address those sitting further back.

- Repeat the exercise with the pupils standing and ask them to comment on how they felt as listeners in this less comfortable situation.

- From this initial modelling it is worth giving the pupils the chance to try out their voices in the space and listen carefully to how it sounds.

While the drama studio is unlikely to have many desks as ready resources, it is likely to have the facility to use lighting to create different contexts for speaking. Separating presenters from audience with different kinds of light generates new challenges and discussion on the experience for both speakers and listeners; as they will soon discover, standing in a sharp spotlight can feel very lonely and intimidating. It is difficult to connect with an audience that you know is there but that cannot be seen clearly. Conversely, backlighting a speaker or lighting him or her from below tends to have a disconcerting effect on the audience.

Pupils will be excited by the opportunity to experiment with a microphone and soon discover how it not only amplifies the volume but also accentuates all the little coughs, splutters, pauses and stabilisers that regularly pepper everyday speech. Give them the chance to listen to what happens when the microphone is held too close to the mouth and how, by turning their head away without keeping the microphone equidistant from their mouth, words can be instantly lost.

The organisation of technical resources can involve significant preparation. However, incorporating the use of lighting, sound, video and *PowerPoint* equipment allows the teacher to help pupils to relate their work in speaking and listening to the world of media and commerce. Giving the work this sort of relevance and a sense of importance will contribute to the motivation of the pupils.

Organising the pupils

Many teachers rehearse the rules for oral work with pupils at the beginning of each new school year. Once again, the exercise can be made into a speaking and listening activity in itself by getting the pupils to discuss what constitutes effective conditions for different types of talk. The resultant mutually agreed contract is not only a device to be used in classroom and behaviour management but provides a basis for the assessment of listening skills. As with any other discipline, teachers need to establish some sort of baseline assessment of speaking and listening skills.

In England, the Year 7 *Key Objectives Bank* for Objective SL 1, 'Clarify through talk', offers one possible model which results in the establishment of rules for oral work, while providing the teacher with valuable information about the level of the pupils' competence:

> Analyse short extracts from radio or television programmes which feature discussion and debate. Provide a transcript on OHT or handout. Pause the tape at an interesting point and consider how the participants are using talk. Ask the class to identify further key features and annotate the script before more detailed discussion with the whole class. Together, identify and list key dos and don'ts. Ask the pupils to make an advice booklet for other pupils.

(DfES 2002a: 65)

The way pupils will be grouped or arranged in the lesson needs to be planned carefully. Random groups and pairs can be created by numbering or allocating colours to pupils as they enter the class or simply counting them into groups. As the teacher gets to know the class better, groups can be sorted according to confidence, friendship, behaviour issues, motivation and even attendance. Setting a baseline assessment task early on will provide invaluable information for grouping pupils appropriately. While programmes of study do not specify details regarding how pupils should be arranged, attainment targets for speaking and listening tend to emphasise the need for pupils to be able to speak in a range of contexts. Creating a variety of contexts includes more than the issue of grouping, but certainly implies that routinely allowing pupils to work in friendship groups will not provide the breadth of experience necessary. As well as looking for ways to create different groupings within a class, teachers can usefully, on occasion, work with colleagues and mix pupils from other classes in order to broaden the context and provide the more challenging experience of addressing larger groups. Introducing visitors into lessons can also develop motivation and challenge in pupils and enhance their questioning skills and ability to talk comfortably with adults. Examples of good practice include:

- inviting other teachers into class to listen to final presentations;
- inviting in staff such as librarians, teaching assistants, cleaners or school governors to answer questions about themselves and what they do;
- visiting local primary schools and working with younger children, by, for example, reading or telling them stories;
- inviting Year 6 pupils to join Year 7 groups in speaking and listening work as part of their transition process;
- preparing presentations for pupils in other years, e.g. getting Year 11 pupils to discuss their GCSE choices and courses with Year 9 groups or asking Year 8 pupils to present an induction session to new Year 7 pupils;

- inviting trainee teachers to interview pupils and discuss their perceptions of the school;

- preparing presentations for assemblies or school events such as book week or drama evenings;

- using events such as arts or technology week as the basis for speaking and listening work focused on register and subject-specific terminology;

- using video conferencing technology to link with other pupils in different parts of the country and across the world.

Whatever the context, a key aspect of organising the pupils is to ensure they understand the context and purpose of the lesson. Clearly signposting what it is they are going to learn and which skills they are hoping to develop by completing the work helps pupils to focus during the tasks and enables them to assess their own progress. Because pupils spend so much of their time in and out of school speaking and listening, they need clear indicators that what is being addressed in a dedicated speaking and listening activity is qualitatively different from their usual conversational chatter: the issue is not whether they can speak and listen, but how well they can speak and listen in different circumstances, to different people and for different purposes. While most pupils appear happy to spend their time talking, without teacher intervention they are generally very selective regarding whom they talk to. Thus, explaining why they have been placed in particular groups is a crucial part of the lesson in itself.

Finding and using resources

On the surface, finding resources to use in speaking and listening lessons may seem one of the less challenging features for the teacher engaged in developing the oral skills of their pupils. There is a ready supply of material worthy of investigation through talk in newspapers, magazines and books, and on the television and the Internet. However, just as pupils need to be challenged to work with increasingly wide audiences so it must be recognised that, left to their own devices, pupils are unlikely to explore unfamiliar materials to any great extent.

More experienced teachers are likely to have a repertoire of favourite role-plays and decision-making games and it is of course helpful for them to share these with new colleagues. Conversely, most beginning teachers will have fresh ideas that are worth experimenting with and developing further, and there is a wealth of ready made materials to initiate discussion and facilitate speaking and listening lessons on the commercial market. However, although there may be no shortage of potential resources, choosing the right resource for a particular group of pupils needs careful consideration of factors such as the age and ability of pupils, the timing of the lesson and the behaviour patterns of the class, while all the time bearing in mind the desired learning outcome.

There is no sure-fire method of selecting resources but two fundamental questions always need to be asked:

- Is the resource or activity stimulating?

- Is it clear what the pupils will learn by engaging with it?

While many of the commercially produced 'off the shelf' resources present opportunities for pupils to practise speaking and listening, a critical review often reveals that they do not actually *teach* pupils these skills or extend knowledge and understanding of spoken English. Conversely, simply referring to curriculum demands regarding what pupils should be taught may leave teachers uninspired as to how they should do this. In England a considerable number of resources have been developed by the DfES to aid teachers with this problem. For example:

- *Year 7 Speaking and Listening Bank* (DfEE 2001c).

- *Key Objectives Bank for Year 7* (DfES 2002a).

- *Key Objectives Bank for Year 8* (DfES 2002b).

- *Key Objectives Bank for Year 9* (DfES 2002c).

- *Giving a Voice: Drama and Speaking and Listening Resources for Key Stage 3* (QCA 2003).

- And the particularly helpful *Drama Objectives Bank* (DfES 2003).

All of these resources offer examples of how to teach the specific objectives stated in the Key Stage 3 Literacy strategy, suggest further resources and give advice on assessment. In addition, a number of training videos have been produced. Examples of giving and modifying points of view and expressing an argument can be found in the tape 'English Department Training 2001' (DfEE 2001d: Unit 7), while 'English Department Training 2002/03 Year 8' (DfES 2002e: Session 4) includes a short sequence that emphasises teacher modelling and pupil self assessment. What these videos demonstrate is the effectiveness of teachers presenting pupils with an example of the speaking and listening skills they are attempting to teach. Just as an English teacher setting out to teach pupils the art of descriptive writing would usually present examples of the genre from a range of literature, the same process is needed in speaking and listening lessons. In *Sequence for Teaching Speaking and Listening* (DfEE 2001d: Module 7) it is proposed that once the teaching objectives have been made clear to pupils, the next step is to 'provide an example/model of an oral language text type and use in class/group investigation or discussion' in order to help pupils to understand both the conventions of the text type and its purpose. The teacher can then go on to set tasks that enable pupils to rehearse and explore the objective further and so accommodate the skills and knowledge in question.

While the sorts of published materials mentioned above are readily available, collecting examples of actual spoken English can be tremendously time consuming. Clearly, the media offer a rich source of models of spoken English. TV or radio phone-ins, chat shows and news programmes can be used to illustrate accent, dialect and the features of spoken English discussed in Chapter 4. Commercials provide useful models of persuasive language, documentaries of explanatory talk, cookery programmes of instruction, the weather forecast of information and so on. Comparing the same style of programme as it is produced by different broadcasting stations draws attention to the way speech is mediated according to the perceived audience. For example, a class might compare the ways in which guests on Radio 4's 'Woman's Hour' are interviewed with the way in which they are interviewed by 'Steve Wright in the Afternoon' on Radio 2.

It is possible to buy video and audio collections that provide examples of particular forms of spoken English and tapes produced annually by examination boards for departmental moderation of speaking and listening may also usefully be shown to pupils as part of their preparation for assessment exercises. Notwithstanding the bewildering array of published and recorded resources, teachers should recognise the wealth of resources immediately accessible in school. Assemblies, sports days, the dining hall and bus queues can all be put to service in the study of spoken language forms and most staffrooms will yield a range of accents and dialectical variation. Models of negotiating, advising, arguing and hypothesising can be shown to pupils if a teacher prepares and rehearses a carefully planned role-play with another member of staff, such as a trainee teacher, a teaching assistant or a willing sixth former.

Learning to listen

So far this chapter has focused on preparing pupils to speak, almost assuming that the listening will take place as a consequence. However, the ability to listen also involves a range of specific skills. These listening skills are not exclusive to English or drama lessons and it is a reasonable expectation that all teachers play a part in helping pupils develop these skills. In England, the *National Strategy for Literacy across the Curriculum* training pack (DfEE 2001b) contains a whole module on ways of developing listening across subjects and many Key Stage 3 Literacy strategy materials offer several focused exercises to develop listening skills. Believing that in the past the ability to listen has been 'caught, not taught', the Key Stage 3 Literacy strategy extends Bullock's idea of a conscious policy on the part of the teacher to improve children's ability to listen by structuring opportunities within the normal work of the classroom (DES 1975: 527).

To some extent a useful analogy can be drawn between listening and reading. For example:

- Skimming: just as a reader may skim a text to get an overall sense of what it contains, so we sometimes 'skim listen' in order to pick up the gist. The result of 'skim listening' to a weather forecast might be that we gather that tomorrow will be a nice day though we may not recall exactly what the temperature and wind speed will be.

- Scanning: just as we might scan a printed text for particular words, so we can 'scan listen'. An example of this would be listening out for a reference to a particular road or area in a traffic report and effectively blotting out all the other information.

What is apparent from these examples is that listening involves deciding what to listen for. This is contingent on evaluating what it is worth listening for and there are of course a variety of reasons to listen. Just as, at times, readers put aside their facility to analyse style critically in order simply to understand the story that is being told, so we may listen to an oral narrative because we are engaged by the content rather than its form. At other times we listen for character. In this instance, what the character actually says is, for whatever reason, not as important to us as how they say it. Conversely, we may listen for the specific purpose of being critically analytical of content, form, character or the relationship between all three. For example, while listening to a party political broadcast we may simultaneously be identifying the key points of the presentation and matching those to the style of presentation in order to help us determine whether or not we trust the presenter.

Where the parallel between reading and listening breaks down rests in the difference between listening, and listening and watching. This difference needs to be recognised and accommodated in the assessment criteria for listening skills. In both cases assessment is dependent upon the pupils' responses to what they have heard, whether those responses are written or oral. However, as has been argued, the influence of visual signifiers on the interpretation of the sense of what is said and how it is evaluated by the percipient is profound. In order to assess listening skills alone, the teacher would need to select material and prepare activities that completely eradicate visual stimuli: a situation that would require extreme experimental conditions and would be neither appropriate nor possible for the classroom or drama studio. Hence, it will always be important for both teachers and pupils to take account of the visual aspects of the context in which they are working. For example, comparing an audio and a video recording of a party political broadcast will only go a limited distance in throwing this difference into relief, because even when listening to the audio recording pupils will still be in a social setting where the reactions of those around them, what might be happening outside the window and what is of interest on the walls may colour their response. This does not suggest, however, that listening skills cannot be taught or assessed. On the contrary, a fundamental listening skill involves deliberately diminishing the effect of extraneous signifiers in order to focus on what it has been decided to listen for. Humans do have the ability to listen selectively. Just as we often fail to register what the eye actually sees when we are intent on looking for a particular thing, so it is that we can skim and scan sounds purposefully. Conversely, we sometimes miss the sense of what is being said because we are distracted by other aspects of what we are hearing. We only really listen attentively when we have a clear purpose for listening. However, the quality of our listening is also related to the quality of what we are listening to and what we are seeing. In the same way that we tend to lose concentration when watching a worn and fuzzy video, so pupils can switch off if teachers seem to be addressing the whiteboard or something outside the window rather than them, or when they are subjected to any speaker droning on about something of little relevance to them.

There are a number of versatile strategies that can be employed with increasing levels of sophistication to help pupils to hone listening skills and become better able to employ them appropriately in different situations. For example:

- listening triads;

- templates;

- listening frames.

One reason for listening that tends not to be mentioned in curriculum orders and levels of attainment is listening for the aesthetic experience it may provide. Such a notion should not be dismissed as frippery. Many English teachers will justify reading literature on the grounds that it is a pleasurable activity; drama teachers would defend the hours they put into extra-curricular productions on the grounds that they like doing it. People variously feast their eyes on visual stimuli from the paintings of Velasquez or Rothko to fast cars and sunsets. They listen to sounds from rock or classical music to bird song and recordings of steam engines for the sheer pleasure of doing so. People gather at Hyde Park Corner for the pleasure of hearing a good speaker rather than because they want to hear anything in particular being spoken about. And why shouldn't they? In terms of learning and pedagogy, what it is important to remember is that any critical appreciation of art, music, literature or drama is built upon the initial sensate experience it has provided the percipient. Ergo, a critical understanding of oral communication is built on an aesthetic appreciation of what is heard and seen in any given context.

There is no sound in a vacuum and the quality of listening achieved is thus always influenced by the physical environment.

Monitoring progress

Progress and progression are separate but related aspects of the acquisition of knowledge, skills and understanding. Both terms imply movement from one situation to another. Given appropriate criteria the amount of movement made can be measured. What distinguishes the terms from each other is that, in peda-gogical terms, teachers are interested not only in the distance a child travels along a given road (their progress), but also in the increasingly different landscapes and challenges they will encounter along the way (progression).

Ensuring progression

The term 'progression' implies that as pupils move through the school they will gain a breadth and depth of knowledge, skill and understanding. Schools need to demonstrate how such progression is achieved. In England, the National Curriculum Programmes of Study for Key Stages 3 and 4 list what pupils should be taught in relatively broad terms under the headings Speaking, Listening, Group Discussion, Drama, Standard English and Language Variation, but do not pre-scribe how or when different elements of these should be taught. The challenge for teachers is thus to ensure that the order in which they teach different aspects of speaking and listening matches the expectations for achievement proposed for each age group. The Key Stage 3 Literacy strategy is helpful in this respect. It sets objectives into a progressive hierarchy and provides support material that offers guidance on what to teach, what teaching approaches might be taken, what tasks might be set to assess pupils' achievement against the objectives and what per-formance indicators might be applied in the assessments. In Year 7 the emphasis is on teaching pupils to extend their skills and develop their basic understanding of key speaking and listening text types and situations. By Year 8 they are expected to be able to reflect on and evaluate their own and others' performance, and to strive for different effects. In Year 9 they should be able to adopt a more critical stance on their work, as well as continuing to reinforce and extend their skills and confidence, especially when working in less familiar situations (DfEE 2001a: vii).

One way of demonstrating progression is to draw up a curriculum map that shows what aspects of speaking and listening are taught and when. In evolving such a map it should be remembered that many of the objectives for speaking and listening can be addressed in tandem with other work. For example, while studying Robert Swindells's novel *Stone Cold* with a Year 9 group opportunities could be taken to address the following:

- SL 2. Use standard English to explain or justify an idea: pupils are asked to present a short spoken statement regarding what they liked or disliked about the novel.

- SL 7. Identify the underlying themes, implications and issues raised by a talk, reading or programme: pupils work in groups to rank order the issues in the novel or BBC production in order of importance as they see them.

- SL 9. Discuss and evaluate conflicting evidence to arrive at a considered viewpoint: pupils hotseat the character Link about how he feels at the end of the novel when he discovers that Gail is not really homeless but an undercover journalist. They then interview Gail to learn her perspective. A chair is placed at each end of the room to represent each of the characters. Pupils are invited to stand somewhere along a line between the two to indicate where their sympathies lie. From this position a number of pupils are invited to explain why they have chosen to stand where they have.

- SL 13. Develop and compare different interpretations of scenes by Shakespeare or other dramatists: selected scenes from Joe Standerline's play adaptation of the novel are rehearsed with the specific intention of affecting the audience in a given way. Pupils discuss both how the dramatised version differs from the novel and how the presentations elicited particular responses from the audience.

Clearly, co-operation between English and drama departments in drawing up a curriculum map that identifies how each department is covering the objectives will help to ensure that unnecessary repetition is avoided, that the curriculum has breadth and that knowledge and skills are built on systematically.

Progress

The term 'progress' concerns the development made by an individual child in the acquisition of knowledge, skill and understanding. Registering, recording and reporting on such progress in speaking and listening is contingent upon the use of specific criteria. In England, these criteria are provided by the stated Levels of Attainments and GCSE specifications.

In order to monitor progress the teacher needs to be able to identify and evaluate tangible outcomes. Some English teachers, used to marking exercise books and coursework folders against criteria concerning the content and the use of form (for example, spelling, punctuation, grammar and structure), may initially consider the more ephemeral nature of speaking and listening work to present an especially difficult challenge. However, this perception would not necessarily be shared by drama specialists. It is worth considering why this is and what the implications are in terms of ensuring that pupils' progress in speaking and listening is monitored effectively and fairly.

Pupils' progress in drama is commonly considered under the headings 'making', 'performing' and 'responding', though arguments exist in favour of adopting two attainment targets: 'making and performing' and 'responding/ evaluating' (Howell-Meri 2003: 45). In either case, these areas of activity are often interrelated. So, for example, in a role-play, pupils will be generating ideas, expressing them and responding to the response they gain. Similarly, in the production of a play, pupils may be involved in researching, writing and rehears- ing, all of which may require negotiation, discussion and indeed persuasion. The performance of the play will require vocal and physical skill and the ability to respond to each other and the audience. Response and evaluation of a different nature follows: have you ever been backstage and not heard the actors analyse their on-stage experience?

The criteria used by drama teachers to assess and subsequently to monitor progress also involve considering content and form (for example, use of voice, space, gesture and interaction). Seen like this, the outcomes of practical speaking and listening work are just as tangible as those of written work. Indeed, written tasks can be used to confirm the extent to which pupils have understood and appreciated both what they have done and what they have seen and heard others do. Given that the development of listening skills can only be monitored in terms of a listener's responses, written tasks represent an opportunity for quiet pupils to demonstrate their progress in this particular area. If drama teachers are adept at assessing the polysemics of live performance and English teachers have the appro- priate tools for measuring responses, then monitoring pupils' progress in speaking and listening need not present an insuperable challenge for a school in which drama and English teachers can work together.

In monitoring pupils' progress in speaking and listening, video recording examples of pupils' work is particularly worthwhile for two reasons. First, it will allow English and drama teachers to work together and discuss their evaluation of the work against the given criteria from different perspectives. Second, such videos can be shown to the pupils to assist in personal evaluations of their own and others' performances.

Assessing and reporting

Formal assessment of speaking and listening is necessary not simply because it is a statutory requirement but perhaps more importantly because it validates the work in the pupils' eyes and emphasises that they can improve. In England the Teacher Assessment for English at the end of Key Stage 3 must contain a level for speaking and listening, while at GCSE the oral work marks make up 20 per cent of the final GCSE grade.

In England the tools for assessing pupils' progress in speaking and listening are level descriptors at Key Stage 3 and GCSE grade descriptors at Key Stage 4. These descriptors are provided for summarising the pupils' overall achievement at the end of a Key Stage and not intended to measure ability in specific skills during a course. At Key Stage 3 performance indicators have been assigned to each key objective. This helps both the pupil and the teacher to understand exactly what they have to do in order to achieve the objective and provides a simple framework for grading by suggesting that teachers consider whether pupils 'always, sometimes or rarely' show evidence of the given skills and knowledge. In a number of training courses accompanying the introduction of the Key Stage 3 support material, many teachers have reported that the simplicity of this scaling device is particularly useful in helping pupils to evaluate their own progress. This method of assessment changes a summative process into a more formative one, allowing teachers and pupils to identify which areas need targeting for further development.

At Key Stage 4 the skills are defined more specifically since pupils have to be assessed against three triplets of objectives (see Chapter 3, page 23). Though these objectives are still quite broad in their range it is possible to identify progress by comparing different grade descriptors. For example, at GCSE a grade E pupil would use 'straightforward and appropriate language' when explaining, describing or narrating, whereas a grade C candidate would be expected to 'use varied and appropriate vocabulary and expression' (AQA 2002: 54). A pupil hoping to attain an A* when exploring, analysing and imagining will need to 'respond inventively through imaginative explorations', whereas simply to 'respond with understanding to ideas of varying complexity' will only achieve a grade C.

Assessment procedures

The assessment of speaking and listening is most frequently undertaken by a single teacher. This is inevitable, since a good deal of assessment happens as a routine part of a lesson. It is clearly not always necessary to set separate assessment tasks out from the work in progress. For example, in order to discern pupils' ability in discussion the teacher can monitor this simply through listening in while the pupils are at work on a given task. The more assessment can be integrated into the learning process in this way the better. However, in the case of some skills – for example, those involving a presentation – it will be necessary to establish a more formal task. If this is done well then the pupils will enjoy rising to the challenge. However, timing is crucial and both teachers and pupils can feel pressured if insufficient time is allowed for preparation and presentation. There are, though, some guiding principles that can make such formal assessment procedures smoother:

- Inform pupils if a formal assessment is going to take place. Make it clear that the teacher is acting in the role of assessor. Set out the room to facilitate the assessment.

- As a teacher assessing pupils, make sure you have clear understanding of what skills you are assessing. Design an appropriate tick sheet or record form to use during the lesson.

- Ensure that pupils know exactly what is being assessed and what skills the teacher is looking for.

- To ensure accuracy of assessment, keep relevant documents easily accessible during the assessment.

- Select carefully which pupils are going to be assessed and consider the order of the presentations. Sometimes a whole class will be assessed, while at other times it may only be certain groups.

- Whenever possible recruit extra help from teaching assistants or trainee teachers. Make clear to them the context of the lesson and their role while you are assessing.

- Design a written task or a self evaluation exercise for pupils to complete after the assessment, which could provide further information for the assessment.

- Record the marks as soon as possible after the assessment, or preferably mark down an emerging grade while it is taking place.

Even given a clear framework, assessing oral work can be a daunting prospect for many teachers, especially those new to the profession. Consequently, it is crucial to try to gain experience whenever possible by, for example:

- attending departmental training sessions and moderation meetings on speaking and listening;

- visiting other teachers who are conducting speaking and listening and co-assessing, moderating marks together;

- participation on an in-service training course.

Once again, co-operation between English and drama teachers in the assessment of speaking and listening has the potential to be mutually beneficial in terms of professional development, conducive to a more coherent speaking and listening curriculum and ultimately in the greater interests of the pupils' progression.

In public examinations the requirements for the moderation of assessment tasks are established firmly within the specifications. Most usually, teachers are required to moderate a videotape of evidence that the examining board sends to the school and then return their marks to the exam board. A representative from each department is expected to attend the annual standardisation meeting. In the GCSE examination for English an oral assessor will visit the school every three years, though this will become annual if a department's moderation marks are seriously inaccurate. The moderation procedures for drama are similar.

Peer and self assessment

Given that the development of listening skills in particular can only be monitored through the pupils' responses, peer group assessment and self evaluation play a vital part in the assessment process. In a secure classroom environment, pupils assessing the performance of their classmates can provide evidence of their own speaking and listening skills. The benefits and outcomes of this will be greatly enhanced if the pupils are given specific criteria on which to comment. Simply asking them to comment on something they liked and something they didn't like is unlikely to elicit much of an informed judgement or help to strengthen their understanding of either content or form. A more productive way of evaluating performances and presentations is to ask different groups of pupils to focus on specific aspects in advance of watching and listening. For example, the teacher might ask one group to pay particular attention to the way the performers use voice and gesture, a second group might focus on movement and positioning, a third on the way tension was built up and so on. After the performance each group is given just a few minutes to marshal their thoughts before reporting their findings. The teacher can then use further questioning to help the pupils to develop and deepen their responses. The resultant feedback provides useful advice for the whole class. It can sometimes be useful to distil the pupils' comments into a list of 'dos and don'ts' for future reference. The more specific the comments are, the more helpful they will be to individual pupils in their self evaluations.

As with peer assessment, simply asking pupils to comment on things they have liked or think they have done well at is unlikely to provide the teacher with sufficiently specific feedback on how the pupils feel they have progressed. Regularly using the same technique or template for self evaluation is more likely to bore the pupils and result in bland responses. As a result of this many teachers have been innovative in designing ways to make self evaluation part of the pupils' learning. One method is to provide the pupils with a mark scheme and then ask them to award their own work a mark. This in itself will not generate self evaluation unless the pupils are required to justify the marks they have given using the mark scheme criteria and specific reference to their work. This process can be developed so that groups of pupils discuss each other's work and then agree on a mark.

Self evaluation techniques that focus on the skills pupils should demonstrate or develop in a piece of work are particularly helpful in helping them to identify their strengths and weaknesses. For example, a teacher may have set pupils to work on a decision-making exercise and given them the aims of:

- expressing a point of view and justifying it with reasoned detailed argument;
- asking questions to find out information;
- reading out loud the information on their cue card clearly to other group members;
- listening to the views of others and recognising when to compromise.

Setting out these aims before the discussion begins reminds pupils of the purpose of their work. After the work is complete, pupils measure themselves against the aims. On a simple level the teacher could ask pupils to write an evaluation of their work referring to the four aims. Alternatively, the teacher could ask pupils to rank order the four aims, placing the one that they did the best at number one and the one that they did least well at number four. Clearly, the learning process is enhanced when the pupils articulate their reasons for the order they chose. Working in pairs, pupils can evaluate each other in the same way and then compare the rank order and discuss the judgements they made. If the teacher also uses the rank ordering techniques as part of their assessment, valuable discussion can arise from a comparison of the teacher's rank order and that of the pupil.

For pupils unwilling or unable to write lengthy self evaluations, tick charts or sentence starters offer some support. For example, pupils can be read a list of the expected outcomes from a speaking and listening activity and then they circle whether they 'Always/Sometimes/Rarely' achieved the outcome. Alternatively, they could be asked to pick words from a list that best describe how they feel about their work. Frequently used sentence starters include:

- The aspect of this work I enjoyed was . . .
- The hardest thing to do in today's lesson was . . . because . . .
- I felt really pleased when . . .
- It was a difficult lesson so I . . .
- I know I have improved because . . .
- I know I could do better because . . .
- I could work harder on this by . . .
- Next time I do work like this I will . . .
- I would get a higher mark if I could . . .
- In the lesson today, I showed that I could . . .

Asking younger pupils to draw a face and then asking them to explain how the face describes the way they felt about a piece of work gives a quick and varied self evaluation and generates a valid piece of explanatory talk. Whatever method of self evaluation a teacher uses, it becomes most profitable when pupils have to consider how they can improve in the future. The pupil who has drawn a miserable self-portrait should be asked what she could do next time so she would be able to draw a happy face, while the pupil who has awarded herself a grade A could be asked to consider what she must do in the next piece of work in order to maintain the high standard.

Recording and reporting

Having completed an assessment, grades and comments need to be recorded and the pupils are informed of the outcome. Legal requirements may specify that there only needs to be one annual report and just one level or grade recorded, but the reality is that, in order for pupils to progress, they need more regular feedback than this. Certainly, failing to feed back on the outcome of formal assessments will devalue the importance of the work in the pupils' eyes and this may have a significant impact the next time a teacher attempts such an exercise. Furthermore, by not offering specific comments on the work the teacher is missing an opportunity for reflection and target setting. If children are not helped to identify where they are now, they certainly will not recognise where they might go next. What is ultimately needed in a school is a method of record keeping that allows teachers to track their pupils' strengths and weaknesses. Records of individual pupils' progress need to be kept simple and manageable so that they can be readily passed between colleagues and, where appropriate, shared with the pupils, whose self assessments should be an integral part of the record (Figure 8.1).

If a teacher specifies the exact skills she is wishing to assess in a speaking and listening task, then the easier the process of recording becomes. In the model in Figure 8.1 the teacher selects three key skills for each task and records attainment in each. Teachers may devise their own notation, but often a grading system that indicates how well the skill has been demonstrated is the most manageable. For example:

1 Pupil often demonstrates the skill in a confident and appropriate manner.

2 Pupil usually demonstrates the skill in a confident and appropriate manner.

3 Pupil infrequently demonstrates the skill in a confident and appropriate manner.

4 Pupil rarely demonstrates the skill in a confident and appropriate manner.

A cross would indicate zero attainment and an 'A' would note absence.

Register of names	Task: Date:					Task: Date:			
(Teacher must identify skills being asked in activity)	Commitment to work	Skill 1 (e.g. asking questions)	Skill 2 (e.g. using an appropriate vocabulary)	Skill 3 (e.g. sustaining a detailed explanation)		Commitment to work	Skill 1 (e.g. answering questions in detail)	Skill 2 (e.g. giving instructions clearly)	Skill 3 (e.g. reporting back key points)

FIGURE 8.1 A record sheet for recording pupils' progress

Such a recording method has several benefits for the teacher. First, it helps the teacher to gain a profile of the pupil without the need for lengthy notes. Second, it is an easily transferable record that shows not only the pupil attainment but also the work covered. Finally, it highlights the types of skills a pupil has practised and allows the teacher to check for breadth and variety across the speaking and listening work over a period of time.

CHAPTER

9

Speaking and listening in classroom practice

Warm-ups and starter activities

Voice and breathing exercises

Good use of the voice is dependent upon good muscle control as much as anything else and like any other muscles the tongue, lips and throat need to be exercised. Breath control is also an essential element of speaking clearly. The following exercises are simple ways of warming up the voice. With all of them, it is important for the class to be standing up in a relaxed way with arms hanging loosely at the side.

- Take in a deep breath through the nose, hold it for a count of five, then release the breath explosively through the mouth. Repeat this three or four times.

- Imagine that you are holding a small feather above your head. Take in a deep breath through the nose, pretend to release the feather and blow gently out through the mouth to keep the feather floating in the air for as long as possible.

- Take a deep breath through the nose, hold it for two seconds then speak aloud the months of the year as quickly and clearly as you can without taking another breath.

- Take a deep breath through the nose, hold it for two seconds, then count from one to ten in a whisper.

- Stand in a small circle and imagine that you are each holding one end of a bungee rope in both hands. The other end is attached to a ring bolted to the floor in the middle of the circle. Take a deep breath then slowly move out from the small circle stretching the rope and making a Zzzzzzzzzz sound until you have virtually no breath left. Imagine being pulled back into the ring by the elastic, yelling ZAPPPPPPP! as you go.

- Practise individual letter sounds using just one breath for each. For example:

T t t t t t t t t

M m m m m m m m

P p p p p p p p p

A a a a a a a a a

Talk about exactly what you need to do with your lips and tongue to make such sounds clearly.

■ Work with individual letter sound but hang on to the one sound rather than repeating it. For example:

Ohhhhhhhhhhhhhh

Ahhhhhhhhhhhhhh

Uuuuuuuuuuuuuuu

Thhhhhhhhhhhhhhh

Ummmmmmmmm

■ Work with short tongue twisters to focus on articulating vowel and consonant sounds. For example:

Sister Suzie's sewing shirts for soldiers
Such saucy, soft, short shirts for soldiers
Sister Suzie sews
Some soldiers send epistles
Say they'd sooner sleep on thistles
Than the saucy, soft, short shirts for soldiers
Sister Suzie sews.

She's the girl that makes the thing
That drills the hole
That holds the spring
That pulls the rod
That turns the knob
That works the thingumebob.

Other useful tongue twisters can be found in *The Works* by Paul Cookson (2000).

Listening exercises

Teachers often complain that many pupils 'simply don't listen'. Perhaps one of the reasons for this is that some pupils don't know how to listen for different purposes. The following short exercises can be used to help pupils to understand that there are different modes of listening involving a variety of skills.

- Ask the class to stand facing front and explain that the only part of the body they need to move in response to a series of instructions is their eyes. Give them a series of instructions such as this, getting faster and faster in your delivery: 'Look at me, Look left, Look right, Look at the ceiling, Look at the floor, Look right, Look at the door, Look left, Look left, Look right, Look left' etc.

- Think of a location in the school and describe to the class what you would see and hear if you were standing there. Try not to make the information you give them too obvious. How quickly can they identify where you are? Again, this activity can be developed into pairs work.

- A further activity that can be built from this is having one pupil describe to another how to get from the classroom they are in to another point in the building. For example: 'Turn left out of this door. Go down the corridor and turn right at the end. Go straight through the double doors. Walk on for approximately 10 metres. Stop. Turn to your right. What do you see in front of you?'

- Explain to the pupils that in this exercise they will need to listen to a whole piece in order to get the general gist of it. Read aloud an article from the local newspaper but leave out the headline. The pupils listen to the article and then write a headline that they think sums up the story.

- Explain to the pupils that they need to listen for key words. Read aloud an article or short story and ask them to list key words under given headings such as place, character names, main actions, emotions.

- Improvise a talk in which you are trying to explain or describe something that you don't fully understand. Deliberately pepper the talk with stabilisers such as 'um, you know, er . . .' The pupils' job is to disregard the content of the talk and count how many stabilisers you use. Try this again, talking about a different subject, using even more stabilisers and vague language. This time the pupils must try to focus on the content by blotting out the use of stabilisers and vague language.

- This exercise requires a decent sized space such as the drama studio or hall. It requires careful classroom management but if you can trust the group it is challenging and fun. A number of obstacles such as chairs or rostrum blocks are placed in the middle of the room. The pupils work in pairs. Pupil A writes her name on a sheet of paper and gives it to Pupil B. Pupil A then stands at one end of the hall with her eyes shut while Pupil B places the paper somewhere in the room and moves to the other end of the hall. When the teacher says 'Go', Pupil B must call out instructions to his partner to guide her through the maze and retrieve the piece of paper with her name on it. This is noisy, but the point is to try to listen out for one voice amongst all the others.

- Another exercise that requires some space involves asking for two volunteers to be blindfolded. Each is given a tightly rolled up sheet of newspaper. This is their Samurai sword. While the rest of the class sit silently as an audience the two players must stalk each other by listening carefully for any signs of movement. The first one to touch the opponent with the sword is the winner.

- An exercise that can be used to consolidate learning and develop listening is to play Quiz Bingo. Each pupil is given a 'bingo card', which, instead of numbers, has words that are the answers to a range of questions. The teacher asks the question, the pupil has to listen, work out the answer and then mark it off the card. Obviously, the pupil who does this first calls out 'Bingo'.

- A further game with cards that is useful for encouraging listening and consolidating knowledge (of key words, for example) is Sequence Cards. The teacher designs a set of cards with a question (or a definition) on one side and an answer, to a different question, on the other. In class, pupils are given a card each and a pupil starts by reading out the question. The class listens and the pupil who thinks they have the answer on their card calls out. Assuming they are correct, this pupil then reads the question on their card. The chain is now under way and pupils work through the entire set. Teachers can time how long it takes to run through a set of cards and pupils can be given the challenge to complete it more quickly in the next lesson.

- Another challenge is Beat the Teacher. This is where the teacher informs pupils that they are going to make a presentation on a topic, but that some key information is missing. Pupils have to listen carefully and score points for spotting the missing information. Similarly, teachers can read out a passage to pupils which contains errors; pupils have to spot the errors. This is suitable for all ages and the teacher can make the errors as obvious or discreet as appropriate. It is particularly good as a starter or plenary.

- Alternatively, Beat the Teacher can be turned into a class quiz with groups of pupils working in teams. In this situation each team presents material with omissions or errors while the other teams score points by spotting the deliberate mistakes.

- Video resources are useful, but sometimes the picture can be a distraction. Listening to the sound without a picture can encourage listening. It is also a useful exercise to then show the same footage again with the picture and to discuss the differences and what else was communicated by the pictures.

- Listening Frames can take various forms, such as:

    1 A sheet with questions to be answered as a video progresses. The teacher will need to stop the video occasionally to allow the pupils time to complete it.

2   A sheet containing key statements. As the pupils listen to the teacher or a video they have to listen for the key statements. Rather than ticking them off, pupils number the statements as they hear them so that the activity becomes an aural sequencing exercise.

3   Dividing the class into groups and giving them a particular aspect of a programme. During the programme they have to make notes on the aspect they have been given. After watching the groups are jigsawed and each member of the new group reports back on the aspect they noted.

4   Issue pupils with a frame that has columns with headings. As they listen they have to fill in information under the relevant heading.

5   Aural cloze procedures are an alternative type of listening frame. Pupils are given a passage (or possibly a transcript of a recording) with gaps. Pupils have to listen and fill in the gaps.

■   For quick, light hearted fun, Hands Up can be a useful game. Pupils are asked to listen for a word and raise their hands when they hear it. Obviously this can be developed: right hand for one word, left for another, a nod of a head for a third word and stand up for a fourth. If there are too many, though, it can become confusing and riotous.

Small group exercises

The following exercises encourage pupils to play with language on their own. Exercises like these give the teacher an opportunity to listen in on groups and make formative assessments of their speaking and listening skills.

■   Working in groups of four or five, one pupil is given a location to describe; for example, the Cursed Tomb of Queen Naffytutu, Professor Strange's Abominable Laboratory, the Haunted House on Horror Hill. The pupil must start to describe their arrival at the location and proceed to give details of all they see, hear and touch there. They are helped in this by having the rest of their group asking for further details:

'I started walking up the path . . .'
   'What was the path made of? Tell us about the sound your footsteps made.'
   'It was a gravel path and it made a crunching sound. I arrived at the front door and rang the bell.'
   'How big was the door? What was it made of? What sound did the bell make?'

The idea of the exercise is to elicit as much fine detail as possible through questioning but also to allow the storyteller the chance to tell the story.

■   Give small groups a contentious topic and a specified time to discuss it (perhaps just five minutes). At the end of the specified time, the group must agree on what the three strongest points were in the debate.

- Give one pupil in each group a card with a short spiel on it such as may be used by a telephone sales operative. For example:

Good morning. I'm calling from the Hot and Cold Ice Cream Company and I'd like to tell you about the special opportunities we are offering to people in your area. We are the country's leading suppliers of hot and cold ice cream and for this week only we are giving you the chance to come along and try our unique products absolutely free of charge and with no obligation to buy anything.

The pupil delivers the speech to each member of the group in turn, who must react in a different way: cautiously interested, resentful at being disturbed, confused etc. The caller must try to deal with the call receiver as helpfully and tactfully as they can until the point when one or the other decides to bring the call to an end.

Whole lessons and sequences

Radio drama

The aim of these lessons is to help pupils to understand how tone, pitch, volume and pace can be modified to create character and atmosphere. Working within the constraints of radio drama also draws attention to the need to take turns when speaking.

Objectives

By the end of the lessons the pupils should:

- be able to use different vocal traces to denote character and atmosphere;
- be able to present a prepared reading of a radio script;
- understand the constraints that must be adhered to in radio drama.

Lesson 1

1 Pupils are asked to think of a time when their mood changed from boredom to excitement or excitement to fear. In small groups they share their memories.

2 Each group nominates one of its members who, they agree, has described the moment well, and these pupils are invited to retell their stories to the whole class. The listeners are asked to watch and listen for the way the storyteller uses tone, pitch, pace and volume to convey the differences between their mood at the start of the story and the mood at the end.

3 Ask the class how they think drama on the radio is different from other types of drama. It would, of course, be useful to play the class a short extract from a radio drama to give them a reference point.

4   Point out to the pupils that in radio plays:

- there are usually quite a small number of characters in each scene (because listening audiences find it hard to identify more than four or five voices at a time);
- the characters usually need to have distinctive vocal traits (this helps to identify the different characters);
- the characters in each scene need to speak fairly frequently (otherwise the audience wonders what has happened to them or forgets that they are in the scene);
- characters can often be heard remarking on their location and what is happening around them (because there can be no visual information on this);
- parts are often doubled, i.e. the same actors use their voices to portray two or three different characters (simply because it is cheaper to make radio plays in this way).

Ask the pupils why these constraints are typical of radio plays.

5   In groups, pupils are asked to devise a sequence of three scenes that would focus on three contrasting emotions. For example:

- The car journey: (a) initial excitement as a family set off on a day trip; (b) boredom and frustration at being stuck in a traffic jam; (c) fear when the car breaks down on a lonely road on a misty moor.
- The bank raid: (a) boredom as a number of friends wait in a queue at a bank to take money out in order to go to the cinema to see a new film; (b) fear at being held hostage by a group of bank robbers; (c) relief when police free them from the siege.

Lesson 2

1   Having decided on the simple structure of their storyline, pupils decide what sort of characters are going to be portrayed, giving each one a simple 'key'. For example: the whining child, the patient mother, the stubborn teenager, the one who is always a little slow on the uptake, the one who always thinks that their idea is best. These will be the core characters in the drama. The group may also choose to have other characters. For example, in the bank robbery they will probably need to depict the bank robbers and the police. What they will need to remember is that they must vary the use of their own voices by doubling up the parts.

2   Time is then given to the pupils to improvise or write their scenes.

3   If time and facilities allow, groups could record their plays; otherwise they should prepare to present them live. If this is the case they should deliver their

play by standing in a semi-circle as if standing around a microphone stand (use one if you can). The constraints are:

- avoid relying on facial expressions and gestures to convey mood and atmosphere;
- try to always keep the same distance from the microphone;
- avoid making any noises which do not fit the scene – this includes being able to turn the pages of scripts silently.

4 After sharing examples of the work discuss how well groups used their voices to create character and changes in atmosphere. Also discuss how well groups worked within the constraints.

Hitting the headlines

The aim of this sequence of lessons is to investigate how different speech registers are used and what their effect on an audience is.

Objectives

By the end of the lessons the pupils should:

- be able to identify the different components of a news report, and use this knowledge of structure and register to plan and create their own representation;
- be able to select and convey images and information to an audience in a way that stresses their significance;
- be able to reflect on the purpose and effect of their own and other students' planning and presentation using relevant vocabulary.

Content

The frame for this series of lessons is a television news report based on an incident that was reported to Lord Louis Mountbatten by his gardener. Mountbatten himself took the gardener's statement and signed it, saying he had every reason to believe the man's story that he had seen an alien and been hit by a powerful yet unrecognisable force that had knocked him off his bicycle.

For much of the time the pupils work in role as a variety of characters who would contribute to the report. This will involve some of the pupils using discussion to prepare written scripts that will then be presented as formal spoken presentations. Others will study written evidence and use this as the basis for spontaneous talk.

Lesson 1

1 The teacher takes the role of an elderly gardener who tells a tale of a strange thing that has happened to him:

An Eyewitness Account by Mr Peter Stratton

I was on my way to work up at Lord Upton's Estate. Everything seemed the same as it was every morning. I was cycling down the same lane at the same time as I always do.

It was about 8.00 and before you ask I hadn't been drinking. Anyone will tell you that apart from the odd sherry at Christmas I never touch a drop. I'm not the type of person that sees things and I know that I didn't imagine this. It really happened.

I've lived here in Newbury all my life and worked on the estate as a gardener for nearly forty years. Now I know just about all there is to know around these parts. I know who comes and who goes. If anything changes I'm the first to know about it.

So, I was cycling along. It was a clear morning. Quite frosty in fact and there was a bit of mist clinging to the ground. Well, I came around the corner just up Deadman's Lane there, I wasn't going fast or anything, when suddenly I heard this sort of humming sound then this great big silver thing appeared in front of me. It was all shiny and sort of hovering about twenty feet or so above the lane.

I stopped and looked at it long and hard. You could see sort of windows around it. It was like a big fat cigar but a sort of silvery blue colour, all shimmery. Then a long sort of ramp came out of it stretching out down to the lane. Then a couple of figures suddenly appeared at the bottom of the ramp. They were quite small, about the size of my grandson I suppose – he's about ten years old. They had these masks on – bit like the old gas masks but the eye holes were purple and there was a round black hole where their mouth should have been. Perhaps they weren't masks but their natural faces. I can't really say because it was then I started moving towards them to get a closer look. They were about thirty metres away I'd say. Anyhow, as I started moving towards them I suddenly got this terrific shock, like some big fist had punched me right in the chest. It was so hard it knocked me right off my bicycle into the hedge. I wasn't knocked out or anything but I was a bit stunned. Even so I could still see what was going on. These two fellers just seemed to be sucked up into the big cigar thing then I heard this rumbling sound and it just sort of shot off. It was like watching the dot on the television disappear when you turn it off.

Now that's the God's honest truth. You call me a silly old fool if you like but that's what I saw.

2 Having told the story, the teacher invites pupils to ask Peter some questions about his tale.

3 The teacher breaks from role and asks pupils what might have made them believe the character's story. Key words are listed on the white board: tone, eye contact etc.

4 The pupils are placed in threes. A relates Peter's tale as if they have completely believed it. B then relates the tale in a way that makes it clear they have not believed it at all. C relates the tale in as neutral a way as possible.

5 Discuss the different vocal and visual registers used in each retelling. What techniques did the person retelling the tale use to indicate that they believed, disbelieved or had no opinion about Peter's story?

6 Divide class into two groups, Believers and Non-believers. Give a few minutes for each group to formulate reasons for their position then conduct a 'tennis debate' (i.e. the teacher allows only one person to speak at a time before handing over to the other side). It would be useful to use an unplugged hand held microphone to signal this.

7 Explain to the class that they will be working towards presenting a television news report that will be video recorded.

8 Show an example of a pre-recorded report from the local television news. Ideally, the example should have the following elements:

- introduction to the item by a studio-based newsreader;
- report from an 'on the spot' reporter;
- interview with eye witness(es);
- interview with an 'expert' in the field;
- statement made by an official.

Ask the pupils to identify the structure of the news item, what sort of people are involved and what their function is. Display the results as, for example, in Table 9.1.

TABLE 9.1 Example analysis of a news item

Character	Function	Presentation
Newsreader	To introduce the item and give brief details	Calm, serious, talks directly to viewing audience using standard English and, most probably, RP
Reporter	To explain the situation in greater depth from the site	Shows a little emotion e.g. excitement or concern; talks a little more quickly and spontaneously; may seem a little informal in choice of vocabulary; addresses studio newsreader
Eye witness	To give personal account and add a 'human' element, making the item relevant	More informal use of language and greater expression of emotion; perhaps uses regional accent; addresses interviewer/reporter.
Expert	To provide detailed information on the importance of the event	Uses specialist language; 'deliberate' delivery in order to make a point that will increase concern; less obvious audience (unseen interviewer?)
Official	To calm people down, suggest that everything is under control?	May use evasive or ambiguous language; gestures and tone designed to calm; addresses viewing audience

9 Ask the pupils to watch the item again and pay particular attention to the different ways that people speak. For example, how do they use their voice (tone, pitch)? What sort of words do they use (vocabulary)? What sort of gestures and facial expressions do they employ (visual signifiers)? What different effects do they appear to want to have on the viewing audience (sympathy, disbelief etc.)? Record their ideas against the 'cast' of the news item.

10 Tell the class that they will be working in role as a news team handling an exciting and important story. Ask them to imagine what the newsroom might look like. What sort of things would they see there (desks, computers, television monitors, maps on the wall)? What sort of sounds would they hear (telephones ringing, keyboards clattering)? What sort of people might be there (reporters, news readers, typists, messengers)? What might they be doing? Write up as many 'specialist' words as possible so that pupils can refer to them and employ them later.

11 Ask the pupils to create the scene using whatever is available in the classroom. Enter the scene in role as the Chief Editor and call their attention. Explain that news is coming through of a 'Close Encounter of the Third Kind'. Explain that you do not know very much as yet but will try to answer any questions they may have. The purpose here is to heighten the dramatic tension and increase the pupils' sense of role. In terms of speaking and listening, the objective is to encourage them to formulate purposeful questions that build on the information they are acquiring. The teacher, in role as the Editor, should keep answers short, possibly suggesting that they do not know the answer but will expect the news team to investigate the question further.

Lesson 2

The class is divided into five equal groups, i.e. newsroom anchors, on-the-spot reporters, eye witnesses, experts and official spokespeople. Each group is given a task sheet and a variety of resources, such as 'facts' about UFOs, on which to draw in order to tackle the task. For example:

The Newsroom Anchor

Who are you?

You are Sam Smile, the person that the television viewers at home are most used to seeing.

You are friendly and sometimes have a little joke with the viewers. When you are dealing with a serious story you change your voice and facial expression to let the viewers know that it is serious.

Sometimes you have to deal with stories that the people at home will have to make up their own mind about. In these cases, you try to show that you aren't too sure about the real truth of the story.

What do you do?

You work in a television studio. You are part of a team that gathers together the details of stories as they come in.

The team sorts out which stories are worth including in the news bulletin and how much time should be spent on each one. They then write a script (or at least some notes) so that you know what to say once you are 'on air'.

Your task as a newsroom anchor

Work in a group.

Read Peter Stratton's eyewitness account.

Each one of you will have the job of introducing this news story to the audience at home.

You need to: (a) prepare exactly what you will say to introduce the story (you should write this on a large sheet of card so that you can read it when you are 'on camera'); (b) decide how to introduce the 'on-the-spot' reporter (you know this reporter quite well and the audience at home need to feel that you are quite good friends); (c) think of two questions that you want to ask the reporter about what has been going on; (d) when the reporter has finished reporting from the scene, introduce an important expert; (e) introduce an official spokesperson.

Groups work on their own on the tasks. Individuals within each group help each other to prepare a rehearsed presentation in preparation for the following session.

Lesson 3

1 Groups are rearranged so that one pupil from each of the existing groups form a new group. That is, each group has one of each of the following: a newsroom anchor, an on-the-spot reporter, an eye witness, an expert and an official spokesperson. These groups are given some time to rehearse their parts ready for video recording. This will involve negotiating how the links between different locations and speaker are to be made.

2 Groups present their work and each piece is recorded on video. The audience is set the task of noting:

- whether each group used the structure of the sample news item effectively;
- whether the performers used language appropriate to character and context;
- whether the performers spoke audibly and clearly and how else they communicated their message.

The class reflect on the presentations and pupils are asked to produce a written reflection of the project focusing on what they learnt about different modes of speech and the challenges they faced in the different roles.

Having a say

The aim of these lessons is to draw attention to the appropriate use of speech in different situations. This includes using descriptive and narrative voices to build up a sense of location and character and changing the meaning of pieces of texts by delivering them in different ways. The lessons also use a forum theatre technique to structure and conduct an argument.

Objectives

By the end of the lessons the pupils should:

- have made conscious use of speech that is appropriate to different purposes and situations;
- have discovered how use of speech can affect the meaning of texts;
- have worked co-operatively to structure and conduct an argument.

Lesson 1

1 Ask the class to look at the whiteboard and imagine that it is the window of a chemist's shop. What sort of things would they see if they looked through the window? Press the pupils to give detailed descriptions.

2 Explain that, one night, a police patrol car had noticed that some pieces of graffiti had been scrawled on to the window. One of them read: 'Baby rabbits, eyes full of pus, Is the work, of scientific us!' (Spike Milligan). There were other pieces of writing on the window. What did they say? Invite pupils to come and write these on the board around the verse above. Some pupils may write other animal rights slogans, others may be more flippant, but this will be useful later.

3 Describe how, after leaving the chemist's shop, the police apprehended a teenage girl walking on her own. Stopping to ask if she was all right, they quickly become suspicious and ask her to turn out her bag in which – surprise, surprise – they find a can of spray paint.

4 The class need to decide on a name and age for the girl. If space allows, ask the class to stand in a square as if they are the walls of the girl's bedroom. Each pupil is asked to think of something that would be found in the room and mentally devise a line that describes this in neat detail. For example: 'A selection of Body Shop goodies lie scattered on the dressing table.' 'CDs and pop magazines are strewn across the floor.' 'Under the bed, a pile of school books.' 'Six mugs, all half full of long cold coffee, decorate the desk and bookshelves.' It is helpful to 'model' lines such as these. That is, pupils' initial ideas are likely to be more vague and not so economical. Take some of these ideas and fine tune them in order to give the pupils examples of how to make

them punchier and almost poetic. The result is a montage of lines that at once draw a vivid picture of the room and, by proxy, the girl's character. Discuss the effect of the montage and what sort of girl the pupils think they have created.

5 Place a chair in the space that represents the girl's room. Ask the class to imagine who might like to say something to the girl if they had the chance. For example, the chemist, someone who was responsible for some of the other graffiti or her mother. Ask the pupils to think about such a character and what they might say. The task is to design a line that illustrates both who they are and what their attitude to the girl is. Pupils take it in turns to speak aloud to the empty chair, trying to use their voice to portray different characters. Once again, it is helpful to give a few examples: 'I don't know who you are or exactly why you think I am responsible for crimes against animals but I can tell you that it is going to cost me a lot of money to get my window cleaned.' 'Hey, Sarah, you haven't told the cops I was with you, have you? I mean, I only went along for a laugh. You'd better not split.'

Lesson 2

1 Pupils work in small groups to write one of the following pieces of text:

- a note from the chemist that is taped on to the window and addressed to her customers about the graffiti that is spoiling the look of the shop;
- a headline and the first paragraph of a story about the incident in the local newspaper;
- a letter in the local paper that sympathises with the graffiti artists;
- a letter in the local paper that is expressing disgust at the incident.

2 The pieces need to be written in clear handwriting, as each piece is passed on to another group. Their task is to think who might read the piece aloud and in what circumstances. For example:

- the girl's father reads the news item aloud to the girl over the breakfast table;
- some of the graffiti artists read the chemist's note;
- the girl's teacher reads one of the letters in the staffroom.

The groups use the text as a script. The constraint is that they must try to show both who they are and what their attitude is to the piece of writing without adding any dialogue. The characters and situation must become clear through the use of space, gesture and facial and vocal expression alone. Watch some examples and discuss how the audience knew who the characters were and what their attitude was.

Lesson 3

1   Explain that the girl's headteacher has requested that the girl and one of her parents attend a meeting in the school to discuss the graffiti incident. Divide the class into three groups to represent the girl, the headteacher and the parent. Each group needs to discuss what their given character thinks about the forthcoming meeting and decide: (a) what they hope the outcome of the meeting will be; and (b) what they hope to avoid happening.

2   Each group will need to nominate a spokesperson. Three chairs are set up facing each other. The spokespeople will sit on these chairs with the rest of their 'team' sitting close behind them. It is a good idea to have the headteacher sitting in the scene first. The teacher can then act as the head's secretary to announce the arrival of the girl and her parent and usher them into the room.

3   Before the meeting starts, explain to the class that a number of rules will be used to shape the meeting:

- If any of the characters say anything that seems completely unbelievable and out of character then any member of the class can raise their hand and say 'stop'. They must then explain why they have stopped the meeting and suggest what the character could have said that would have been more appropriate to the situation.
- If any team member feels that their character is moving away from what they want and putting themselves in danger of getting what they have decided they do not want, they call 'time out'. The teams then have the chance to hold a quick (and secret) strategy meeting to decide how they might turn the argument in their favour.
- If any of the characters feel they do not know how to respond to a point made by another character they too can call 'time out' and either ask their team for advice or ask to be replaced by another member of the team.

4   In order to spice the meeting or give it a new focus, the teacher might decide to give teams one of the following 'jokers':

- Tell the headteacher that the chemist is chair of the school governors and has promised financial support for the school. She has demanded a written apology or she will withdraw her promise.
- Tell the girl that she learnt the Spike Milligan poem from an English teacher in a recent lesson about animal rights.
- Tell the parent they are standing for the local council and the last thing they need is for their name to be linked with any bad publicity.

Of course, you may add as many jokers of your own devising as you can think of.

5 It is difficult to predict how a debate such as this might end. Sometimes one of the characters will bring it to a natural end by deciding to leave the meeting or perhaps the headteacher decides that enough has been said and calls the meeting to a close. The teacher can always play their own joker if necessary by entering the scene as the secretary and announcing that the headteacher's next appointment is waiting. Either way, at the end of the meeting there will be a great deal to discuss:

- How well did each character do in achieving their objective for the meeting?
- To what extent was the language used in the scene appropriate? That is, did the talk fit the characters and the situation?
- What other jokers might have affected the outcome of the meeting?

Further development

A number of other scenes might be explored as extension tasks in this drama. For example:

- In pairs, pupils improvise two contrasting scenes. The first depicts the conversation in the car between the girl and her parent on the way to the meeting. The second shows them talking on the way home.

- Working in small groups, the pupils show how the girl is received by the other graffitists. Some might, like her, be committed to the cause of animal rights, while others are simply having a laugh.

- In pairs, pupils improvise the scene in which the headteacher is trying to find out from the English teacher just what the lesson on animal rights entailed.

It's what you wear

This short sequence of lessons draws on the pupils' everyday experiences of language in school and in the media and draws parallels between the two in order to foster a better understanding of description, explanation and persuasion as modes of speech.

Objectives

By the end of this series of lessons pupils will have learned:

- to recognise spoken description, explanation and persuasion;
- to analyse the impact these forms can have on a listener;
- to use these forms effectively to engage and stimulate an audience.

Lesson 1

1 In friendship pairs, the pupils complete three short tasks:
- describe their favourite outfit to their partner;

- explain why it is their favourite outfit;
- persuade their partner to wear their favourite outfit.

2 The pupils present one of the three conversations and are invited to comment on the conversations by considering:

- What differences did they notice in the language used between the descriptions, explanations and persuasions?
- How did the body language and tone of voice alter between the descriptions, explanations and persuasions?

3 Tell the pupils you have just overheard snippets of a number of conversations during break time. Read out some of these snippets and ask pupils to decide whether they are description, explanation, persuasion or a mixture.

- I can't let you copy my homework. Last time you did she spotted it and she'll know again.
- Your exercise book is better than mine. It's so neat and clean.
- My mum won't let me go. She says I'm too young.
- Give us some of your chips. I'm starving.
- That's the new pupil there wearing trainers and a hooded top.
- Don't forget to meet us at break so we can pay in our trip money.
- Can I borrow your pen, please? I really need it. Lend us your pen, mate.
- I hate science. The rooms always stink and they're hot.
- I couldn't do my homework last night because we had a power cut.
- My dad's given me some money for some new shoes. These ones are too tight and I've got horrible blisters.
- I've got a detention tonight and it's so unfair.
- My detention last week was because I was caught cheating in the maths test.
- Can you get my bag from room 4? I'll be late if I go over there now.
- Tell miss I've gone to see the nurse. Tell her for me, she'll believe you.
- I've left my PE kit at home so I don't have to do hockey.

4 Distribute copies of the lines above among the class, one line to each pair of pupils. Ask the children to devise a short conversation that includes the line. Ask them to:

- experiment with different ways of saying the line;
- think about how body language and tone of voice may affect the meaning.

5 Allow a selection of pupils to present their work. After they have done so, draw out conclusions about the relationship between these modes of speech and the way in which they can be mixed or influenced by use of gesture, tone, facial expression, stance etc.

6 As a plenary, ask each pupil to write down one thing they have learned about spoken description, explanation and persuasion.

For homework, ask pupils to think about an assembly they have really enjoyed or a teacher who always gives good assemblies. Ask them to make a list of reasons why the assembly or teacher was good.

Lesson 2

1 As a starter and in order to recall the key features of spoken description, explanation and persuasion, ask pupils to read out some of the sentences they wrote at the end of last lesson (without revealing the subject, of course) and ask other class members to decide whether the sentence defines description, explanation or persuasion.

2 In groups, pupils are given an advert from a magazine for a fashion item. Each group prepares a short presentation that explains how the advert attempts to persuade the reader to buy the product. They should consider whether the advert is descriptive or explanatory as well as persuasive.

3 Show the class a TV commercial, preferably for a fashion product to maintain continuity of topic. Show the advert once then ask the pupils to watch it again. A third of the class try to spot descriptive elements, another third listen out for explanations and the final third watch and listen for persuasive elements. Each group feeds back their observations to the whole class.

4 Allow for a third viewing and then ask pupils to assess whether they consider the commercial to be successful and why. Draw out the use of description and explanation as persuasive techniques. Conclude this section by asking pupils to watch a commercial at home (or listen to one on the radio) and to analyse in what ways the advert is persuasive and how dependent it is on description and explanation.

5 In the final part of the lesson, refer to the homework on assemblies set in the last lesson. In pairs ask pupils to share their thoughts on assemblies and pose the question: how similar are assemblies to TV commercials?

6 Conclude the lesson by drawing up a list of factors that create a successful assembly.

Lesson 3

1 Start the lesson by watching a video of a teacher giving an assembly. Structure this section by giving pupils a listening frame. The frame should focus pupils' attention on:

- how the teacher presents her material;

- the types of language the teacher uses;
- the use of voice;
- the use of body language;
- the interaction with the audience;
- the use of audio visual props, if appropriate.

Stop the video and replay it as necessary to allow pupils to analyse the assembly.

2 In pairs, ask pupils to evaluate the assembly and measure it against the list of 'what makes a good assembly' drawn up in the last lesson. Take feedback and note the main points on the board.

3 Put pupils in groups of five or six and give them the following 'memo':

To: Year 8 Pupils
From: Headteacher

Urgent

There have been some bad instances of bullying in recent days. The cause of this bullying seems to be FASHION. Pupils are being bullied for not wearing the 'right' designer labels or for wearing clothes considered to be unfashionable. To combat this, I want pupils to organise a series of assemblies on the theme of 'It's not what you wear'. The aim of the assembly is to:

- describe how the bullying is causing a problem in the school;
- explain why people should not be victimised because of the clothes they wear;
- persuade the bullies to stop their anti-social behaviour.

The assembly should last for at least five minutes and no longer than ten.

4 Tell the pupils they have to devise a suitable assembly and give them the remainder of the lesson to devise this by referring to their notes on 'good assemblies'.

5 As a plenary to conclude the lesson, each group presents a one-minute taster of the work in progress.

Lesson 4

During this lesson, the pupils present their assemblies. Some form of evaluation is necessary to consolidate their learning. Ideally, the assemblies could be video recorded so that they could be watched and analysed. Evaluation of the assemblies needs to focus on:

- How closely does the assembly match the criteria for a good assembly drawn up by the class?

- How much of the assembly is description, explanation and persuasion and how effective is this in communicating the message of the assembly to the audience?

- How did the visual presentation of the assembly impact on the audience (presentation and body language of the speakers as well as any visual aids)?

- How successful do they think the assembly would be in combating the type of bullying referred to in the 'memo', and why?

References

Ackroyd, J. (2001) Acting, representation and role. *Research in Drama Education*, 6(1), 9–22.

Alexander, R. (2002) Dialogue of cultures: international perspectives on oracy. In *New Perspectives on Spoken English*. London: QCA.

Arts Council England (2003) *Drama in Schools*. London: ACE.

Arts Council of Great Britain (1992) *Drama in Schools*. London: ACGB.

Assessment and Qualifications Alliance (2000) *GCSE Drama* (3241). Guildford: AQA.

Assessment and Qualifications Alliance (2002) *GCSE Drama* (3702). Guildford: AQA.

Barnes, D. (1988) The policy of oracy. In M. Maclure, T. Phillips and A. Wilkinson (eds), *Oracy Matters*. Milton Keynes: Open University Press.

Barnes, D. *et al.* (1976) *From Communication to Curriculum*. Harmondsworth: Penguin.

Bearne, E. (1995) *Greater Expectations: Children Reading and Writing*. London: Continuum.

Bernstein, B. (1990) *The Structuring of Pedagogic Discourse, Volume 4*. London: Routledge.

Berry, C. (1973) *Voice and the Actor*. London: Harrap.

Blair, J. and Fenton, N. (1978) *The Biko Inquest*. London: Rex Collings.

Bond, E. (1966) *Saved*. London: Methuen.

Bourdieu, P. (1990) *Homo Academicus*. Stanford, CA: Stanford University Press.

Bourdieu, P. (1991) *Language and Symbolic Power*. Cambridge: Polity Press.

Brecht, B. (1963) *The Life of Galileo*. London: Methuen.

Britton, J. (1972) *Language and Learning*. Harmondsworth: Penguin.

Bruner, J. (1996) *The Culture of Education*. Cambridge, MA: Harvard University Press.

Carter, R. (ed.) (1990) *Knowledge about Language and the Curriculum*. London: Hodder and Stoughton.

Carter, R. (2002) The grammar of talk: spoken English, grammar and the classroom. *Language Issues*, 14(2), 2–8.

Carter, R. and Adolphs, A. (2003) Creativity and a corpus of spoken English. In S. Goodman, T. Lillis, J. Maybin and N. Mercer (eds), *Language, Literacy and Education: A Reader*. Stoke-on-Trent: Trentham Books.

Chekhov, A. (1996) *The Cherry Orchard*, trans. P. Gems. Cambridge: Cambridge University Press.

Churchill, C. (2002) *A Number*. London: Nick Hern Books.

Clipson-Boyles, S. (1998) *Drama in Primary English Teaching*. London: David Fulton Publishers.

Coffin, C. (2001) Spoken English and the question of grammar: the role of the functional model. Unpublished paper presented to the Qualifications and Curriculum Authority seminar, 'Speaking and Listening'.

Cookson, P. (2000) *The Works*. London: Macmillan.

Daniels, H. (2001) *Vygotsky and Pedagogy*. London: Routledge Falmer.

DES (1963) *Half Our Future* (the Newsom Report). London: HMSO.

DES (1975) *A Language for Life* (the Bullock Report). London: HMSO.

DES (1988a) *English for Ages 5 to 11*. London: HMSO.

DES (1988b) *Report of the Committee of Inquiry into the Teaching of the English Language* (the Kingman Report). London: HMSO.

DES (1989) *Drama from 5 to 16*. London: HMSO.

DfEE (1998) *The National Literacy Strategy: Framework for Teaching*. London: DfEE.

DfEE (1999a) *The National Curriculum: Handbook for Secondary Teachers in England*. London: DfEE.

DfEE (1999b) *History: The National Curriculum for England*. London: DfEE.

DfEE (1999c) *Mathematics: The National Curriculum for England*. London: DfEE.

DfEE (1999d) *English: The National Curriculum for England*. London: DfEE.

DfEE (2001a) *The Framework for Teaching English Years 7, 8, 9* (DfEE W019/2001). London: DfEE.

DfEE (2001b) *National Strategy for Literacy across the Curriculum* (DfEE 0235/2001). London: DfEE.

DfEE (2001c) *Year 7 Speaking and Listening Bank* (DfEE 0141/2001). London: DfEE.

DfEE (2001d) *Sequence for Teaching Speaking and Listening* (DfEE 0234/2001). London: DfEE.

DfES (2002a) *Key Objectives Bank for Year 7* (DfES 0207/2002). London: DfES.

DfES (2002b) *Key Objectives Bank for Year 8* (DfES 0206/2002). London: DfES.

DfES (2002c) *Key Objectives Bank for Year 9* (DfES 0203/2002). London: DfES.

DfES (2002d) *Key Stage 3 English: Roots and Research* (DfES 0353/2002). London: DfES.

DfES (2002e) *English Department Training Year 8* (DfES 01313/2002). London: DfES.

DfES (2003) *Drama Objectives Bank* (DfES 0321/2003). London: DfES.

Dixon, J. (1988) Oral exchange: a historical review of the developing frame. In M. Maclure, T. Phillips and A. Wilkinson (eds), *Oracy Matters*. Milton Keynes: Open University Press.

Eagleton, T. (1991) *Ideology*. London: Verso.

Edexcel (2000) *GCSE Drama* (1699). London: Edexcel.

Ellis, V. (2002) *Learning and Teaching in Secondary Schools*. Exeter: Learning Matters.

Evans, L. and Nash, J. (1987) *Lives Worth Living*. In C. Reddington (ed.), *Six TIE Programmes*. London: Methuen.

Fleming, M. (2001) *Teaching Drama in the Primary and Secondary School*. London: David Fulton Publishers.

Ginsborg, J. (2002) Early years reading and writing hampers speech. *Times Educational Supplement*, 4 January.

Hall, L. (1997) *Spoonface Steinberg*. London: BBC.

Hargreaves, D. (2001) A capital theory of school effectiveness and improvement. *British Educational Research Journal*, 27(4), 487–503.

Harland, J. (2000) *Arts Education in Secondary Schools: Effects and Effectiveness*. Slough: NFER.

HMI (1979) *Aspects of Secondary English*. London: HMSO.

HMSO (1943) *Report of the Committee of the Secondary Schools Examination Council on Curriculum and Examinations in Secondary School* (the Norwood Report). London: HMSO.

Honey, J. (1997) *Language Is Power*. London: Faber.

Horner, S. (2002) Move to end neglect of speaking skills. *Times Educational Supplement*, 11 January.

Howell-Meri, M. (2003) In praise of drama in schools. *Drama*, 2(10), 44–5.

Jeffcoate, R. (1992) *Starting English Teaching*. London: Routledge.

Kempe, A. (2003) The role of drama in the teaching of speaking and listening as the basis for social capital. *Research in Drama Education*, 8(1), 65–78.

Knowles, L. (1983) *Encouraging Talk*. London: Methuen.

Kowzan, T. (1968) The sign in theatre. Reprinted in E. Aston and G. Savona (1991), *Theatre as a Sign System*. London: Routledge.

Labov, W. (1970) *The Study of Non-standard English*. Champaign, IL: National Council of Teachers of English.

Maclure, M., Phillips, T. and Wilkinson, A. (eds) (1988) *Oracy Matters*. Milton Keynes: Open University Press.

McPherson, C. (1997) *The Weir*. London: Nick Hern Books.

Mercer, N. (2000) *Words and Minds*. London: Routledge.

Nichols, P. (1971) *Forget-Me-Not Lane*. London: Faber and Faber.

Nicholson, H. (1999) Talking in class: spoken language and effective learning. In E. Bearne (ed.), *Use of Language across the Secondary Curriculum*. London: Routledge.

Nystrand, M. and Gamoran, A. (1991) Instructional discourse, student engagement and literate achievement. *Research in the Teaching of English*, 25, 261–90.

O'Rourke, P. and O'Rourke, M. (1990) English teachers and the history of English. In R. Carter (ed.), *Knowledge about Language and the Curriculum*. London: Hodder and Stoughton.

O'Toole, J. (1992) *The Process of Drama*. London: Routledge.

Oxford, Cambridge and RSA (2000) *GCSE English* (1916). Cambridge: OCR.

Pateman, T. (1991) *Key Concepts*. London: Falmer Press.

Perera, K. (1987) *Understanding Language*. Sheffield: National Association of Advisers in English.

Qualifications and Curriculum Authority (2000) *English: The National Curriculum for English*. London: QCA.

Qualifications and Curriculum Authority (2003) *Giving a Voice: Drama and Speaking and Listening Resources for Key Stage 3* (QCA/03/1075). London: QCA.

Reza, Y. (1996) *Art*. London: Faber and Faber.

Ridley, P. (1998) *Sparkleshark*. In *Two Plays for Young People*. London: Faber and Faber.

Robinson, K. (2001) *Out of Our Minds*. Oxford: Capstone.

Rowe, A. (1975) *English Teaching*. London: Hart-Davis Educational.

Russell, W. (1984) *Our Day Out*. London: Methuen.

Secondary Heads Association (1999) *Drama Sets You Free*. Bristol: SHA.

Standerline, J. (1999) *Stone Cold*. Cheltenham: Stanley Thornes.

Storey, D. (1970) *Home*. London: Samuel French.

Styan, J. L. (1975) *Drama, Stage and Audience*. Cambridge: Cambridge University Press.

Swindells, R. (1993) *Stone Cold*. London: Hamish Hamilton.

Theatre Workshop (1965) *Oh What a Lovely War*. London: Methuen.

Trudgill, P. (1975) *Accent, Dialect and the School*. London: Edward Arnold.

Vygotsky, L. (1962) *Thought and Language*. Cambridge, MA: MIT Press.

Vygotsky, L. (1978) *Mind and Society: The Development of Higher Psychological Processes*. Cambridge, MA: Harvard University Press.

Wesker, A. (1962) *Chips with Everything*. London: Jonathan Cape.

Wilkinson, A., Davies, A. and Berrill, D. (1990) *Spoken English Illuminated*. Buckingham: Open University Press.

Wilkinson, A. *et al.* (1965) *Spoken English*. Birmingham: University of Birmingham.

Index